PENGUIN BOOKS

DOUBLE TALK

Manjula Padmanabhan (b. 1953) is a Delhi-based writer and artist. Her comic strips appeared weekly in the *Sunday Observer* (Bombay, 1982-86) and daily in the *Pioneer* (New Delhi, 1991-97). Her books include *Hot Death, Cold Soup* (Kali for Women, 1996), *Getting There* (Picador UK, 1999), *This is Suki!* (Duckfoot Press, 2000) and *Kleptomania* (Penguin Books India, 2004). *Harvest* (Kali for Women, 1998 and subsequently in three separate international anthologies), her fifth play, won the 1997 Onassis Award for Theatre. Manjula has illustrated twenty-four books for children including her own novels, *Mouse Attack* and *Mouse Invaders* (Macmillan Children's Books, UK, 2003, 2004).

PENGUIN BOOKS

USA | Canada | UK | Ireland | Australia
New Zealand | India | South Africa | China | Singapore

Penguin Books is part of the Penguin Random House group of companies whose addresses can be found at global.penguinrandomhouse.com

Published by Penguin Random House India Pvt. Ltd
4th Floor, Capital Tower 1, MG Road,
Gurugram 122 002, Haryana, India

Penguin Random House India

First published by Penguin Books India 2005

10 9 8 7 6 5 4 3 2

ISBN 9780143032663

Printed at Repro India Limited

DOUBLE TALK

MANJULA PADMANABHAN

PENGUIN BOOKS
An imprint of Penguin Random House

INTRODUCTION

Suki's story begins in mid-1982, in the pages of Bombay's *Sunday Observer*. She was twenty years old, sassy and unruly. Though she started out as my alter-ego, she quickly established her own persona: while I struggled to support myself on my earnings as a freelance illustrator and occasional journalist, she was mostly unemployed; I lived precariously as a paying guest, while she paid little attention to money, household chores or any other practical matters. In fact, it was Suki who paid *my* rent by ensuring a trickle of income every month.

The strips in this book represent two-thirds of those that appeared in print during Suki's Bombay years. I will always be hugely grateful to Vinod Mehta, founder-editor of India's first Sunday newspaper, for being so generous towards her. He put up with her antics with no complaint, from her scruffy early drawings to her always panicked last-minute arrivals at the press, and placed no restrictions on what she said, did or looked like. Such freedom is rare in journalism. It tremendously boosted my confidence as a cartoonist and illustrator.

Seeing these strips in sequence now reminds me of how much Suki changed between the first strips and the last, in late 1986. The early frames are packed tight with details and I used a .02 Rotring pen to write the speech bubbles, making the text almost impossible to read. But then the paper began to introduce colour sections. I could no longer produce the strips on time if I wanted to maintain the same level of detail. Meanwhile, the discipline of having to meet my deadlines every week gradually resulted in a drawing style that was smoother and more precise. Rather than draw the frame-lines free-hand, I used a ruler to get them straight: as so many well-organized people had discovered before me,

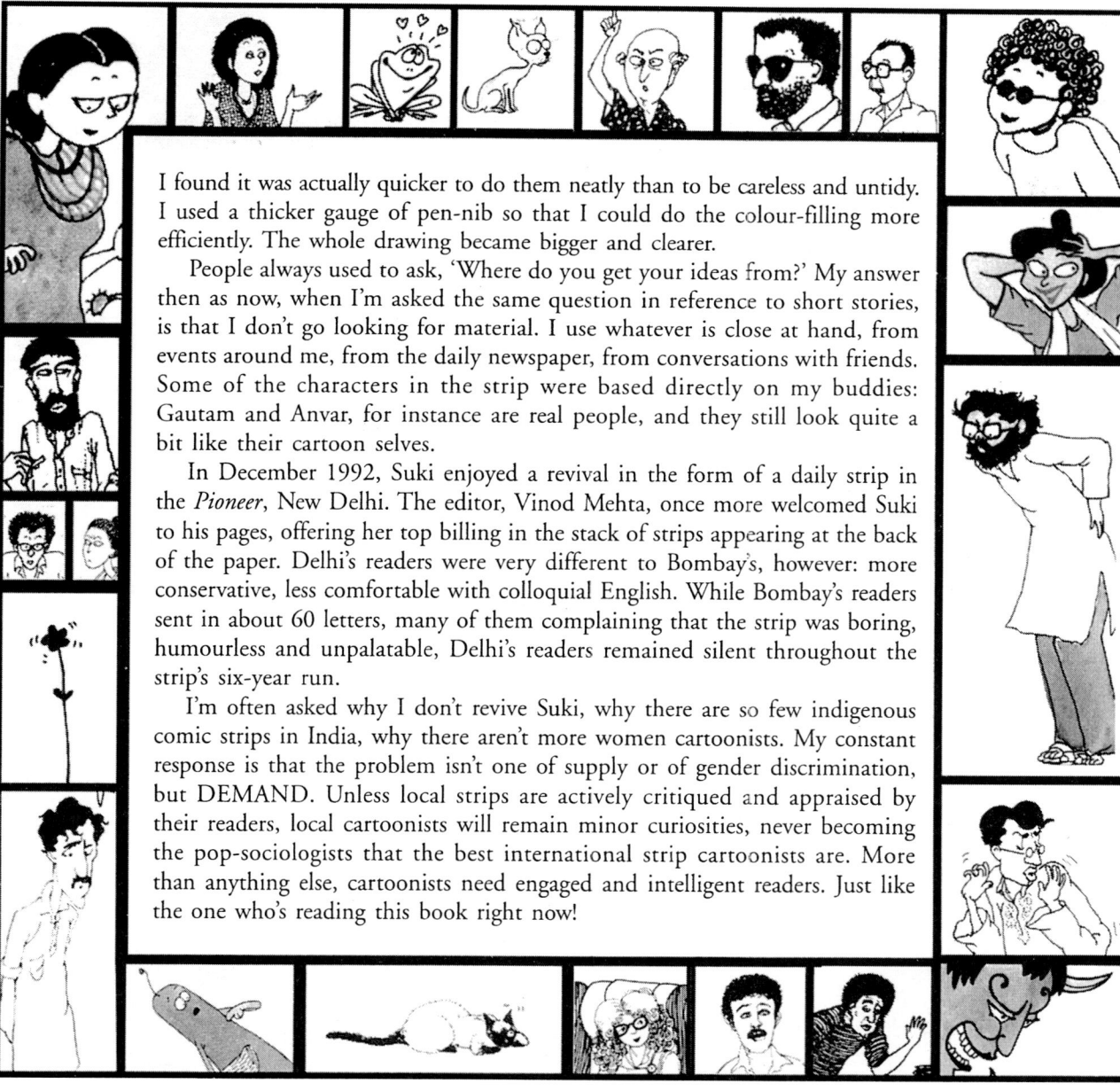

I found it was actually quicker to do them neatly than to be careless and untidy. I used a thicker gauge of pen-nib so that I could do the colour-filling more efficiently. The whole drawing became bigger and clearer.

People always used to ask, 'Where do you get your ideas from?' My answer then as now, when I'm asked the same question in reference to short stories, is that I don't go looking for material. I use whatever is close at hand, from events around me, from the daily newspaper, from conversations with friends. Some of the characters in the strip were based directly on my buddies: Gautam and Anvar, for instance are real people, and they still look quite a bit like their cartoon selves.

In December 1992, Suki enjoyed a revival in the form of a daily strip in the *Pioneer*, New Delhi. The editor, Vinod Mehta, once more welcomed Suki to his pages, offering her top billing in the stack of strips appearing at the back of the paper. Delhi's readers were very different to Bombay's, however: more conservative, less comfortable with colloquial English. While Bombay's readers sent in about 60 letters, many of them complaining that the strip was boring, humourless and unpalatable, Delhi's readers remained silent throughout the strip's six-year run.

I'm often asked why I don't revive Suki, why there are so few indigenous comic strips in India, why there aren't more women cartoonists. My constant response is that the problem isn't one of supply or of gender discrimination, but DEMAND. Unless local strips are actively critiqued and appraised by their readers, local cartoonists will remain minor curiosities, never becoming the pop-sociologists that the best international strip cartoonists are. More than anything else, cartoonists need engaged and intelligent readers. Just like the one who's reading this book right now!

HELLO THERE!!! I'M YOUR FRIENDLY NEW CARTOON STRIP, FULL OF LAUGHS, JOKES, RIBALD STORIES AND LOTS, LOTS MORE..... FUN! FUN! FUN! ALL THE WAY!
HELLO THERE!!! I'M YOUR FRIENDLY NEW CARTOON STRIP, FULL OF LAUGHS, JOKES, RIBALD STORIES AND LOTS, LOTS MORE..... FUN! FUN! FUN! ALL THE WAY!
HELLO THERE!!! I'M YOUR FRIENDLY NEW CARTOON STRIP, FULL OF LAUGHS, JOKES, RIBALD STORIES AND LOTS, LOTS MORE..... FUN! FUN! FUN! ALL THE WAY!
?!
HUMOUR? RIBALD?? FUN???
WHAT'S ALL THIS JUNK?
HELLO THERE!
MY CONTRACT WAS FOR A SERIOUS COMIC STRIP, A SOCIALLY COMMITTED COMIC, STUDIOUS, SOBER, INTELLECTUAL, BORING...... IN SHORT, ANYTHING BUT FUNNY!
....SO I GUESS I'LL JUST HAVE TO SPEAK TO MY SCRIPT-WRITER ABOUT IT...
OFFICE OF THE SCRIPTWRITER
KNOCK KNOCK
NOW SEE HERE ABOUT THIS SCRIPT!!! I THOUGHT WE HAD AN UNDERSTANDING ABOUT IT? HMMMM? I MEAN, WHAT'S ALL THIS ABOUT ....UM HUMOUR ...AND... ...UH...
...AH.... .....THAT IS..... .....UM ...I... UH...
YOU MEAN....
YASSS?
WE'RE THE SAME PERSON??
YOU BETTER BELIEVE IT, KID!
CHEER UP! THINGS COULD BE WORSE
HOW?
LIKE..... YOU COULD HAVE WRITTEN THE SCRIPT..

SOME OF YOU DUMMIES HAVE WRITTEN IN TO SAY THAT YOU DIDN'T UNDERSTAND LAST WEEKS CARTOON
GOD! ARE SOME PEOPLE DUMB!!
I MEAN, IT'S SO OBVIOUS—!
IT STARTED WITH THIS GIRL, RIGHT? ME, IN FACT.
AND THEN THERE WAS THIS SPEECH-BUBBLE, RIGHT?
AND THE SPEECH-BUBBLE DID NOT MATCH MY ACTIONS —
RIGHT?
SO THEN THIS CARTOON CHARACTER —MYSELF, IN SHORT— DECIDES THAT SHE MUST MEET HER SCRIPTWRITER —REMEMBER THAT?
THEN, SHE —I MEAN, ME —UH— I DISCOVER THAT THE SCRIPT-WRITER IS MYSELF, RIGHT?
AND I DON'T GET ON WELL WITH MYSELF —NO, WAIT, THAT'S NOT WHAT I MEANT—
YOU SEE, I DON'T AGREE WITH MY SCRIPT-WRITER
BUT WE ARE THE SAME PERSON
SO-I-UM DON'T AGREE WITH MYSELF??
NO ..... THAT'S NOT IT.....
WELL, LOOK AT IT THIS WAY— THE SCRIPT-WRITER IS MY ALTER EGO AND SHE HAS— I MEAN, I HAVE A DISAGREEMENT WITH—
NO THAT'S NOT IT EITHER!
HOW ABOUT: THE SCRIPT-WRITER IS THE REAL CHARACTER, AND I AM JUST A COMMERCIAL BREAK?
NO— THAT'S NOT IT—
MAYBE I'M THE REAL ONE AND SHE—
WELL...I DON'T KNOW....
BUT IT'S VERY SIMPLE WHATEVER IT IS.....

DUMMIES! JERKS! NINCOMPOOPS! TROGLODYTES!
NOBODY UNDERSTANDS ME!!
NOBODY LIKES MY COMIC STRIP!!
UH.. MISS? ...UH... AHEM!
I CAN'T STAND IT!!!
...EXCUSE ME... UM... ...MISS?... ...HELLO?...
WHAT IS IT?!! CAN'T YOU SEE I'M DEPRESSED??!
UHH... THE EDITOR SENT ME, MISS, TO ASK IF YOU COULD STOP SCREAMING, PLEASE?
...UM... AND, PERHAPS, A LITTLE LESS ABUSE? OUR READERS ARE VERY SENSITIVE, HE SAYS.
THEY WON'T LIKE BEING CRITICIZED.
THEY MIGHT WITHOLD THEIR SUBSCRIPTIONS, AND THEN WE'D ALL BE OUT ON THE STREETS.
ANYTHING ELSE??
YES... UM... ...HE SAYS... COULD WE HAVE A FEW JOKES?
YOU KNOW... ...JUST A LITTLE... ...HUMOUR?
THEN MAYBE A FEW VEILED REMARKS ABOUT THE POLITICAL SITUATION
AND A SHORT RESUMÉ OF THE HUMAN CONDITION
...AND...
...SO ON...
IS THAT ALL?
...YES... I THINK ...SO...
MY LIFE IS LIKE A DARK, DARK, CLOUD...

WE PROTEST
HEY!
WHAT ARE YOU DOING IN MY COMIC STRIP?
WHO ARE YOU?
MADAM. I AM A MEMBER OF YOUR READING PUBLIC.
I'M HERE TO PROTEST ABOUT YOUR SO-CALLED COMIC STRIP
HOW DARE YOU TRESPASS ON MY PROPERTY?
WE PROTEST
FOR THREE SUNDAYS, YOU HAVE BORED US WITH YOUR NEUROTIC OBSESSIONS, YOUR INCONSEQUENTIAL VIEWS!
SO FAR, NOT EVEN A SINGLE WORD ABOUT SOMETHING MORE INTERESTING
- SUCH AS?
- SUCH AS: OUR GREAT AND GLORIOUS CULTURAL HERITAGE!! OUR TEMPLES! OUR ZOOS!! OUR POLITICIANS!!!
WE PROTES
IN FULL COMPENSATION, WE, THE PUBLIC DEMAND A CABARET — SONGS, ROMANCE AND DIRTY JOKES TOO, IF YOU CAN MANAGE IT
BUT-BUT-THIS IS A COMIC STRIP...
...NOT A HINDI FILM!
MADAM! SURELY YOU RECOGNIZE THAT ALL OF LIFE IS A HINDI FILM? EVENTUALLY?
WE PROTEST
BUT I CAN'T DO A CABARET — IT WOULD BE SO DEMEANING
I'M A FEMINIST
I CAN'T JOIN THE FLESH-TRADE I CAN'T SELL MY BODY!
I CAN'T COMPROMISE MY PRINCIPLES
AND BESIDES — WHAT WILL MY MOTHER SAY?
I'M SORRY, MADAM: THE NEEDS OF THE PUBLIC MUST BE CATERED TO—
IF NOT IN REAL LIFE THEN—ATLEAST IN A COMIC STRIP!!
I CAN'T I CAN'T I CAN'T I CAN'T I CAN'T
OUR LIVES ARE SO BLEAK—
WE FACE, AS PART OF OUR DAILY REALITY, RIOTS, STRIKES, ENDLESS QUEUES, CROWDED BUSES, BURSTING TRAINS, SHORTAGES OF MILK, OF BREAD, OF LIFE'S NECESSITIES, HIGH RENTS, LOW PAY, UNSCRUPULOUS EMPLOYERS, DISHONOURABLE OFFICIALS BUREAUCRATIC RED-TAPE, POWER CUTS, WATER CUTS, GAS CUTS, DEAD TELEPHONES— AND NO TELEPHONES AT ALL— RECESSION, DEPRESSION, REPRESSION, UNEMPLOYMENT, CROWDED SCHOOLS CROWDED COLLEGES SOCIAL VIOLENCE, GANG WARFARE, PETTY LARCENY, DISHONESTY, RELIGIOUS BIGOTRY, COMMUNAL HATREDS RACIAL TENSIONS
TELL ME, FRIEND
HOW MANY CABARETS......?

OOOOOHH
I FEEL SO SILLY
IT'S NOT JUST THE OUTLANDISH COSTUME, THE GARISH MAKE-UP, THE INDECENT EXPOSURE—
IT'S THE REVERSAL OF SOCIAL STATUS THAT HURTS THE MOST
I LOOK LIKE A CHEAP TWO-BIT DANCING GIRL
A HOURI!
A VOLUPTUARY!
A SEX OBJECT!
MY FRIENDS WILL SHUN ME I'LL BE SCORNED; RIDICULED; DENIED CLUB MEMBERSHIPS
—OUTCASTED FROM DECENT SOCIETY—
—STONED IN PUBLIC—
ABANDONED BY MY FRIENDS—
OSTRACIZED HOUNDED OUT REVILED HATED ABUSED SPAT UPON DISCARDED
IN FACT.... HERE COME A COUPLE OF MY FRIENDS NOW
HI!
HI...
HI!
HOW'VE YOU BEEN?
GREAT!!
ALRIGHT! AND YOU?
OH.... NOT TOO BAD....
HOW'S WORK?
ALRIGHT.... A BIT BARE.....
GOOD. GOOD. READ ANYTHING INTERESTING?
YEAH— BELLYDANCING MADE SIMPLE—
UNH-HUNH
SEEN ANY MOVIES?
YES.... CABARET
BEEN DOING ANYTHING NEW?
HOW WAS YOUR STAY IN MADRAS?
ALRIGHT....
WELL, I'VE CHANGED MY CLOTHES...
GOOD. GOOD.
OK— LET'S HAVE DINNER OUT NEXT WEEK
WELL..
I— UH—
YEH— GOTTA RUN NOW— SEE YOU SOON—
UMM....
BE GOOD
BYE
BYE
BYE....
BYE....
I FEEL ROBBED OF MY RIGHTFUL SHARE OF ANGUISH

I SEE YOU'RE STILL WEARING THAT RIDICULOUS COSTUME -
TAKE IT OFF AT ONCE
I GOT USED TO WEARING IT -
RIGHT NOW? WITH THE READERS WATCHING??
YOU'RE JUST PLAYING UP TO YOUR ROLE AS A SEX OBJECT
UHHHH.... WHO - ME?
YES!! - AND AFTER ALL THAT FUSS YOU MADE, LAST WEEK - HOW COME, ALL OF A SUDDEN, YOU STARTED TO LIKE THIS BIZARRE MODE OF DRESS?
WELL, TO BEGIN WITH, IT'S VERY COOL IN SUMMER
GOD! WHAT'S HAPPENED TO YOU!!
YES??
NOTHING. WHY?
YOU USED TO BE AN ARDENT FEMINIST
I STILL AM
THEN - HOW CAN YOU DRESS IN THIS BLATANTLY SEXIST FASHION???
I'M SO LIBERATED THAT IT DOESN'T MATTER ANYMORE WHAT I WEAR
HOW CAN YOU SAY THAT!
STOP BEING CALLOUS
HMMPHHH!
EASY - I JUST OPEN MY MOUTH AND VIBRATE MY VOCAL CORDS
THAT WAS SUPPOSED TO BE FUNNY
I NOTICE YOU'RE NOT LAUGHING
THIS IS NO LAUGHING MATTER!
HALF OF HUMANITY IS OPPRESSED SUBJECTED AND HUMILIATED BY THE OTHER HALF
AND ALL YOU CAN DO IS LAUGH
ISN'T THAT ONE OF THE BIGGEST PROBLEMS WITH FEMINISM?
YES
NO
THEN WHAT ARE YOU DOING??
I AM TRYING TO BRING SOME LIGHTNESS TO AN OTHERWISE SERIOUS SUBJECT
WHY?
BECAUSE IN THE END WOMEN AND MEN HAVE TO SHARE THIS PLANET PEACEFULLY......
- EVEN WHEN MEN MAKE LIFE IMPOSSIBLE FOR WOMEN?
.....IS THERE A CHOICE?
Manjula

HELLO WORLD!!
ISN'T IT GOOD TO BE ALIVE?
DID YOU WAKE UP AND HEAR THE BIRDS SINGING? SEE THE SUN SHINING?? SMELL THE —
— WELL, LET'S LEAVE THE SMELLS OUT
BREATHE THE —
— WELL, ALRIGHT, WE'LL LEAVE OUT BREATHING, THE AIR'S TOO POLLUTED FOR THAT —
WALK OUT INTO THE —
WELL, NO, I GUESS THERE'S NO OPEN SPACE LEFT IN WHICH TO WALK
READ THE —
— UHHHH, NO, LET'S NOT EVEN THINK ABOUT THE DAILY NEWS —
LOOK OUT OF YOUR WINDOW AT THE —
NO, IT'S ALWAYS BETTER WITH THE CURTAINS DRAWN.....
OH WELL — WHO NEEDS REASONS?
HELLO WORLD, ANY WAY!!
Manjula

THERE'S SOMETHING STRANGE ABOUT THIS THING WE'RE SITTING ON
I THINK YOU SPEND TOO MUCH TIME WORRYING ABOUT STRANGENESS
BUT LOOK– YOU'RE SITTING ON AN EDGE WHILE I'M SITTING ON A PLANE
I MEAN, WHAT DOES IT LOOK LIKE ON THE OTHER SIDE?
OOOPS!
!
THAT'S OFTEN WHAT HAPPENS WHEN YOU EXAMINE THE BASIC STRUCTURES OF YOUR OWN REALITY TOO CLOSELY...
Manjula

8.

WHAT'S THAT??
ZIP!
SPROING!
CREEP
CREEP
CREEP
SWISH!
!
Manjula

HI-
DO YOU HAVE A LIGHT?
YES,
BUT I'LL HAVE — TO HUNT FOR IT IN MY HANDBAG
I'M SURE I HAD A BOX OF MATCHES IN HERE
THEY'RE THERE, I KNOW THEY'RE THERE, I CAN ALMOST FEEL THEM....
MAYBE IN THIS POCKET? NO? IN THIS ONE THEN — NO — PERHAPS IN THE INNER POCKET — NO
AHA! I SEE IT!
HERE YOU ARE ...
WHAT'S THE MATTER?
IS SOMETHING WRONG?
NOTES
Manjula

ONE BAR OF CHOCOLATE, PLEASE
TWO RUPEES
THIS NOTE IS TORN— I CAN'T ACCEPT IT
NO IT ISN'T!
YES IT IS — LOOK, HERE AND HERE....
BUT I DON'T HAVE ANY MORE SMALL CHANGE
DO YOU HAVE POSTAGE STAMPS?
WILL AN AIR-MAIL FORM DO?
NO, I DON'T NEED AN AIRMAIL FORM — BESIDES, IT'S THE WRONG AMOUNT
HOW ABOUT FIVE RUPEES?
SORRY— YOU KNOW HOW IT IS WITH CHANGE THESE DAYS—
THE ONLY OTHER NOTE I HAVE IS A FIFTY
WE ACCEPT THOSE
THANK GOODNESS IT WASN'T A HUNDRED—
Manjula

SUDDENLY, FOR NO REASON AT ALL, I FEEL LIKE SCREAMING!
EEEYAHH
YIYIYIYIEEE
ARGGGGHH
A OOO
OOOOEEEYIEI
EEAAARRHE
iiiiEEEK!!!!!
THAT FELT GOOD!

WHAT'S THAT OVER YOUR HEAD?
HUH?
OH- I DON'T KNOW - IT LOOKS LIKE A LIGHT BULB
WHAT'S IT DOING THERE?
WELL, IT'S OVER YOUR HEAD...
HOW WOULD I KNOW?
MAYBE WE SHOULD TURN IT ON AND SEE WHAT HAPPENS
YES, I CAN SEE A SWITCH - HERE, LET ME TURN IT ON
CLICK!
HEY!
I'VE JUST GOT AN IDEA FOR MY COMIC STRIP!
HERE'S HOW IT WILL START—

DO YOU BELIEVE IN GOD
NO
BARRROOOM!
RUMBLE! RUMBLE!
REALLY? YOU TRULY DON'T BELIEVE!
NO, I DON'T!
CRACK!
WELL! DO YOU BELIEVE NOW??
NO!
POW!!
NO!
ZAP!
...AND NO AGAIN!!
BUT WHY DON'T YOU BELIEVE IN HIM?
BECAUSE HE'S SUCH A BULLY!

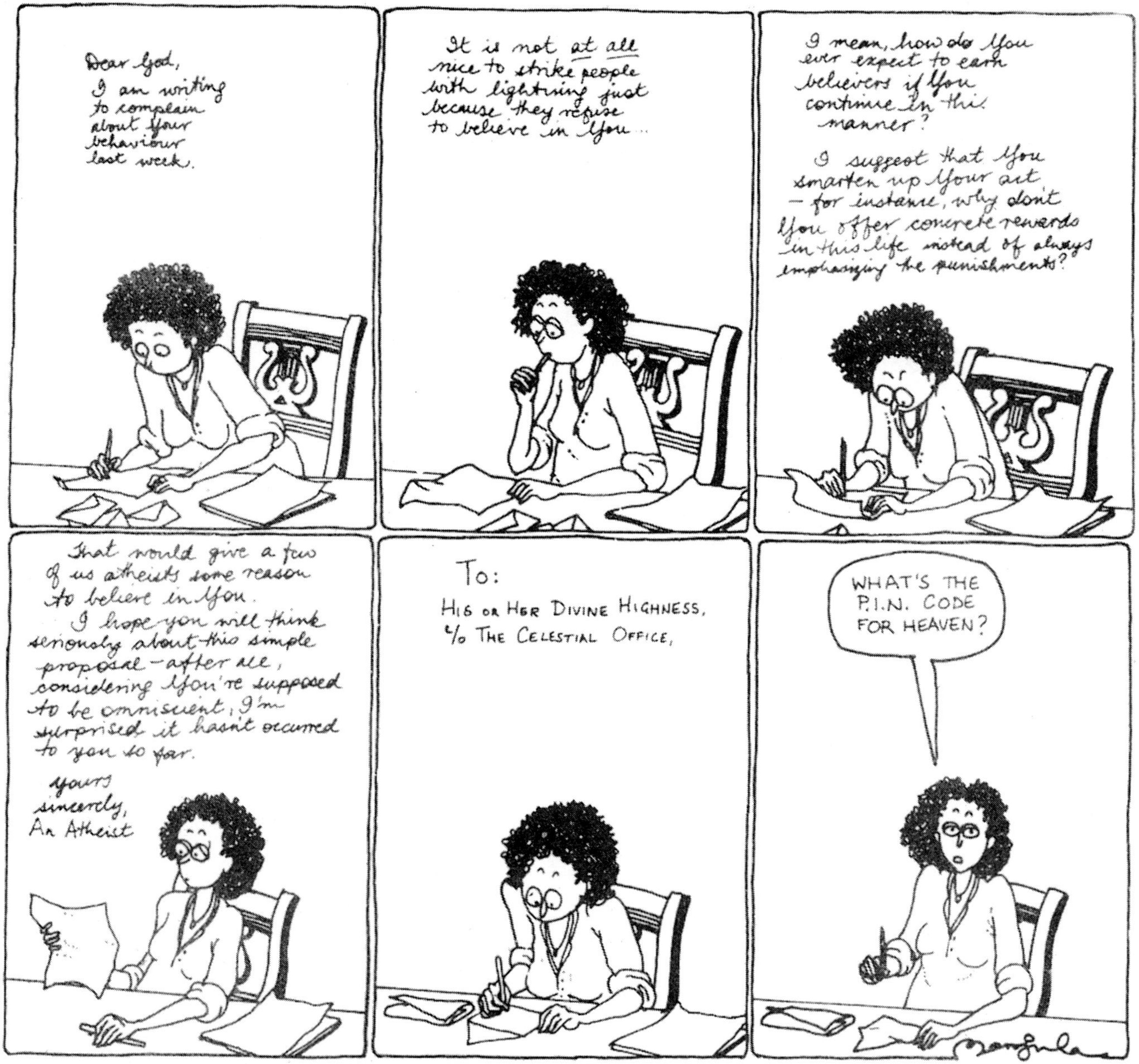
Dear God,
I am writing to complain about Your behaviour last week.
It is not at all nice to strike people with lightning just because they refuse to believe in You...
I mean, how do You ever expect to earn believers if You continue in this manner?
I suggest that You smarten up Your act – for instance, why don't You offer concrete rewards in this life instead of always emphasizing the punishments?
That would give a few of us atheists some reason to believe in You.
I hope you will think seriously about this simple proposal – after all, considering You're supposed to be omniscient, I'm surprised it hasn't occurred to you so far.
Yours sincerely,
An Atheist
To:
His or Her Divine Highness,
c/o The Celestial Office,
WHAT'S THE P.I.N. CODE FOR HEAVEN?

DID YOU WRITE YOUR LETTER TO GOD?
YES...
HOW DID YOU SEND IT?
I MADE A FIRE OUT OF POSTAGE STAMPS, INCENSE AND SEALING WAX, AND THEN I BURNT MY LETTER
HOW WILL YOU KNOW THAT HE'LL GET IT?
BUT DO YOU THINK YOU'LL BE ABLE TO RECOGNIZE IT?
I THINK HE'LL PROBABLY SEND ME A SIGN—
I'M SURE IT WON'T BE HARD—
REALLY? HOW ARE YOU SO SURE?
BECAUSE...
CRACK!!
...SO FAR, HE'S BEEN FAIRLY UNSUBTLE....
Manjula

WHAT ARE YOU DOING?
I'M CARVING AN IMAGE OF GOD FOR MYSELF
WHY BOTHER? THERE ARE SO MANY READY-MADE ONES TO CHOOSE FROM ALREADY—
YES-BUT I DON'T LIKE ANY OF THE STANDARD MODELS, SO I THOUGHT I'D MAKE MY OWN
WHAT WILL YOUR GOD LOOK LIKE?
I'M UNDECIDED— IT COULD BE NEO-REALIST WITH POST IMPRESSIONIST UNDERTONES OR BASIC LATE SURREALIST...
I DIDN'T MEAN WHAT STYLE OF ART!—
I MEANT, WILL YOUR GOD LOOK HUMAN OR ANIMAL OR VEGETABLE
OH— IT'LL BE ABSTRACT. YOU SEE, I STILL DON'T REALLY BELIEVE IN GOD, SO IT MAKES SENSE IF MY IMAGE OF HIM OR HER OR IT REMAINS UNDEFINED....
BLAMM!
PERHAPS WHAT I REALLY NEED IS A GOOD LIGHTNING CONDUCTOR....
Manjula

HEY! HOW COME YOU'RE PACKING?
I'M GOING ON A SHORT TRIP
WHERE TO?
I'M NOT ABSOLUTELY SURE YET BECAUSE I HAVEN'T GOT ALL MY VISAS – BUT MY FIRST STOP IS AT LONDON
LONDON?!?
YES – WHY ARE YOU SURPRISED?
WHY WOULD ANY SELF-RESPECTING INDIAN WANT TO GO TO ENGLAND?
WHAT'S WRONG WITH ENGLAND?
WELL!!! EVERYONE KNOWS THAT THE ENGLISH ARE RACIST BIGOTED AND INTOLERANT
REALLY?
–WORSE THAN INDIANS?

HELLO!
HELLO -
GETTING OFF AT LONDON?
YES - AND YOU?
ME, TOO
WHAT DO YOU DO?
I WORK IN A COMIC STRIP
IN A COMIC STRIP?
YES - IT APPEARS IN A WEEKLY PAPER IN BOMBAY
OH.
AND WHAT DO YOU DO?
ME? I'M AN EXTRA-TERRESTRIAL, DISGUISED AS A HUMAN, COLLECTING RESEARCH MATERIAL ABOUT THIS PLANET
I SEE
SOME PEOPLE TELL ALL KINDS OF SILLY FIBS JUST BECAUSE THEY'RE WITH STRANGERS
SOME PEOPLE TELL ALL KINDS OF SILLY FIBS JUST BECAUSE THEY'RE WITH STRANGERS
Manjula

HERE I AM, IN QUEUE AT THE IMMIGRATION COUNTER AT HEATHROW
ONE HEARS AWFUL STORIES ABOUT ASIANS BEING MISTREATED BY IMMIGRATION AUTHORITIES HERE
PERSONALLY I FIND IT AN ORDEAL
I START TO STAMMER I GET TONGUE-TIED NERVOUS AND HYSTERICAL I FEEL INTIMIDATED AND LOSE CONFIDENCE IN MYSELF
EVEN THOUGH I'M HERE ON A SHORT VISIT, THE IMMIGRATION OFFICIAL MAKES ME FEEL LIKE A DIRTY BROWN RAT, SNEAKING IN TO STEAL JOBS AND GAIN IMMIGRANT STATUS
THEY ARE INSULTING IN ALL KINDS OF SMALL WAYS: THEY ASK EMBARRASSING QUESTIONS, THEY DON'T LOOK YOU IN THE EYE, THEY ANSWER ABRUPTLY—
NEXT!
IMMIGRATI
HOW LONG DO YOU PLAN YO STAY?
-UM-
ALRIGHT.
SIX MONTHS' VISITOR'S ENTRY PERMIT
STAMP!
IMMIGRATI
ATION
THEY'VE GROWN MORE SUBTLE WITH THEIR INSULTS....
Manjula

THEY SAY THAT INDIANS ABROAD DO NOT GREET THEIR FELLOW INDIANS WHEN THEY MEET IN THE STREETS
WELL, I'M GOING TO CHANGE THAT- WHEN I SEE OTHER INDIANS, I'M GOING TO SMILE AND BE FRIENDLY
HERE COMES ONE NOW
!
WHY IS THIS STRANGE WOMAN LEERING AT ME?
A PAKISTANI PERHAPS.....

ONE DAY AT INDIA HOUSE, London....
ER- EXCUSE ME, I HAVE A PROBLEM GETTING A VISA -
ALRIGHT- GO AND SEE MR MUKHERJEE, DOWN THE CORRIDOR, LAST DOOR TO THE LEFT
ENQUIRIES
VISA SECTION
I'D LIKE TO SEE MR MUKHERJEE PLEASE?
WHICH MR MUKHERJEE??

HERE I AM, IN BOMBAY AGAIN—
THE BEST PART ABOUT GOING AWAY IS..... COMING BACK!
—MEETING ALL YOUR FRIENDS CATCHING UP ON GOSSIP RECONNECTING THE TRAILING WIRES—
OH LOOK! HERE COMES SOMEONE I KNOW
HI!
HELLO! I'VE JUST GOT BACK!!!
OH??
YOU'VE BEEN AWAY?

WHAT ARE YOU DOING?
PEOPLE COMPLAIN THAT THEY CALL ME BUT MY PHONE DOES NOT RING SO- I'M GOING TO TRY HYPNOSIS ON IT
HOW TO HYPNOTIZE ANYTHING
YOU ARE FEELING SLEEPY YOUR EYES ARE CLOSING YOU ARE GOING TO RING YOU WILL RING YOU WILL RING YOU WILL RING
MIRROR
YOU WILL....HMMMM?? WHA - WHAT'S GOING ON? I'M - I'M FEELING SLEEPY MY EYES ARE CLOSING I'M-I'M GOING TO....TO....
....RING! RING! RING-RING! RING-RING! RING-RING! RING-RING! RING-RING! RING!
!
RING-RING! RING-RING! RING! RING!
HEY! IS SOMETHING THE MATTER??
RING-RING! RING-RING! RING'RING!
CAN YOU HEAR ME? CAN YOU SPEAK TO ME? CAN YOU GET A DIAL TONE??
RING- RING-RING
THESE TELEPHONES NEVER WORK...
RING-RING! RING-RING! RING-RING! RING-RING!

MY GOD! WHAT'S WRONG WITH HER?
SHE WAS TRYING TO FIX HER TELEPHONE BY HYPNOTIZING IT, BUT, BY ACCIDENT, HYPNOTIZED HERSELF
NOW SHE THINKS SHE'S A TELEPHONE
RING RING!
HAVE YOU CALLED FOR HELP??
I WASN'T SURE WHETHER TO CALL THE DOCTOR OR —BOMBAY TELEPHONES
LOOK!! SOMETHING NEW HAS HAPPENED!
I HEARD A CLICK, JUST LIKE A 'PHONE BEING PICKED UP....
CLICK!!!
SHE'S TRYING HARD TO SAY SOMETHING!!
SOUNDS LIKE A TERRIBLE LINE.....
BLEEP
DIT-DIT-DIT
CLICKACLICKACLICK
SCREEEECH
CLICKACLICKACLICK
SQUAWK
EERRRKK
CLICKACLICKACLICK
SQUEEEEE
CLICKACLICKA
OKAY—IT'S CLEARING UP—I CAN HEAR A FAINT VOICE IN THE DISTANCE—THERE, I ALMOST GOT IT—SAY IT AGAIN JUST ONCE MORE, LOUDER NO, I CAN'T UNDERSTAND—OH—!
WHAT IS IT? WHAT IS IT?
"SORRY" SHE SAID, "WRONG NUMBER..."
Manjula

CHURCHGATE
STATION?
NO, CLOSE BY –
HOW CLOSE?
HALF WAY DOWN TO MARINE DRIVE – LISTEN, ARE YOU GOING TO TAKE ME OR NOT?
NEAR AMBASSADOR HOTEL, RIGHT?
NO, ON THE OTHER SIDE OF THE ROAD – COULD WE GET STARTED PLEASE?
WHICH SIDE OF THE ROAD?
I'LL GET DOWN NEAR GAYLORDS AWRIGHT? NOW, CAN WE LEAVE?? THERE'S SOMEONE WAITING FOR ME AT HOME –
GAYLORDS, HUH? WHAT'S THAT – A RESTAURANT?
YES! LET'S GO!!! I'M ALREADY HALF AN HOUR LATE –
SORRY, I CAN'T TAKE YOU –
AND WHY NOT??
THE FARE'S TOO LOW? YOUR SHIFT'S DUE TO CHANGE? YOU DON'T LIKE RESTAURANTS? YOU ONLY TAKE FOREIGNERS? YOU HATE WOMEN PASSENGERS?
YOU'RE AN UNDERCOVER AGENT FOR BE.S.T.? YOU DON'T DRIVE ON SUNDAYS? YOU'VE RUN OUT OF CASSETTES FOR YOUR STEREO SYSTEM?
NO – I'M OUT OF GAS –
Manjula

OH
WHAT?
I DIDN'T KNOW YOU WORE GLASSES
I DON'T— I WEAR CONTACT LENSES
REALLY? DON'T THEY HURT?
NOT AT ALL — MINE ARE SOFT LENSES
THEY ARE MARVELLOUS— YOU CAN HARDLY FEEL THEM AT ALL, YOU CAN WEAR THEM FOR THE WHOLE DAY AND THEY NEVER FALL OUT OR FLY OFF—
THEY'RE VERY FINE AND DELICATE AND ABSOLUTELY TRANSPARENT — THEY LOOK JUST LIKE THESE DROPS OF WATER IN THE SINK—
IN FACT THERE'S ONLY ONE BIG PROBLEM—
WHAT'S THAT?
FINDING THEM—
Manjula

ONE CONA COFFEE PLEASE
I'LL HAVE A STRAWBERRY MILK SHAKE
1500 –
SIP
!
2500 –
SIP
3500 –
SIP
WHAT ARE YOU DOING?
COUNTING E. COLI –
Manjula

THE EXERCISES IN JANE FONDA'S WORKOUT BOOK ARE SUPPOSED TO BE REALLY EFFECTIVE FOR LOSING WEIGHT
OOOH! I'M VERY STIFF!
OOoFF!! -2-3-4-
OUCH! -6-7-8
YAH! -10-11-12
EEECH! -14-15-16
YOWW! OWW! OWW!
AAARGH! AAARGH! AAARGH! AAARGH!
WELL? HAVE YOU LOST ANY WEIGHT?
OH SURE!
'SPECIALLY MY THROAT...

WOW! WHAT HAPPENED TO YOU?
I WAS WALKING ALONG THE ROAD AND I FELL INTO A POTHOLE
HOW YOU EXAGGERATE! WHAT YOU MEAN IS, A MANHOLE
—NO, IT WAS A POT-HOLE: IT DIDN'T HAVE A COVER
SO WHAT? THE MANHOLES DON'T, EITHER
BUT IT WAS WIDE AND IN THE MIDDLE OF THE ROAD AND FULL OF SLUSH
AH! THEN IT WAS A TELEPHONE CABLE BEING LAID
NO— THE CABLE LAYING SEASON IS SUMMER— IN THE MONSOON IT'S POT-HOLES
NONSENSE! IT WAS EITHER CABLES OR BURST SEWERS —DID YOU NOTICE A STENCH?
BUT ISN'T THAT ALWAYS THERE, FROM THE GARBAGE LEFT UNDISPOSED?
THE GARBAGE IS NEVER DISPOSED OF— IT'S ONLY REARRANGED
WELL ANYWAY— I FELL INTO A POT-HOLE!!
SERVES YOU RIGHT— FOR JAY-WALKING—
BUT THERE'S NO PLACE ON THE SIDEWALKS BECAUSE OF THE VENDORS!
ALRIGHT! WHAT WERE YOU DOING OUTSIDE IN THE FIRST PLACE?
—OUR BUILDING HAD BEEN EVACUATED FOR FEAR OF A HOUSE COLLAPSE....
Manjula

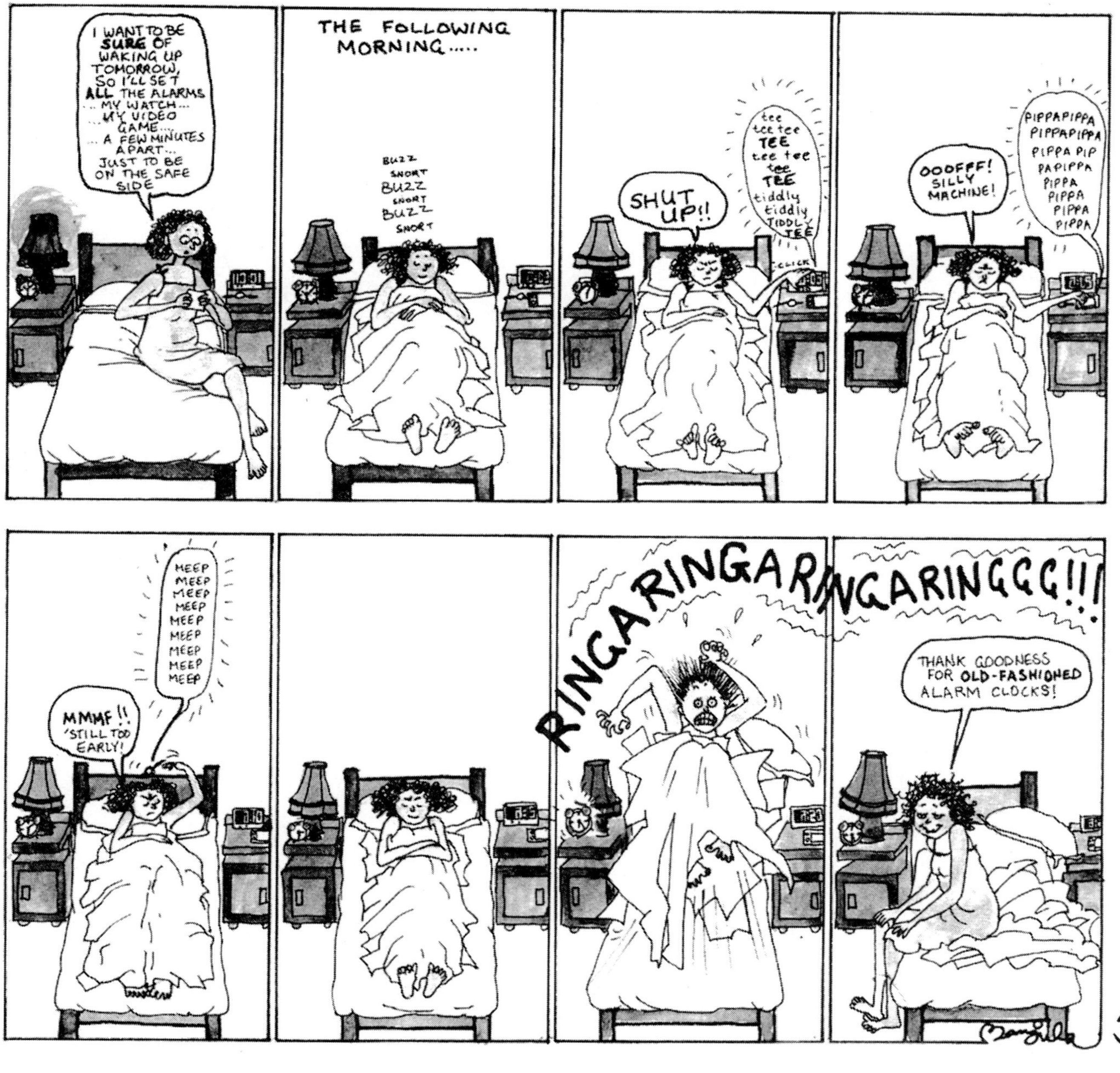
I WANT TO BE SURE OF WAKING UP TOMORROW, SO I'LL SET ALL THE ALARMS ... MY WATCH... ...MY VIDEO GAME... ... A FEW MINUTES APART... JUST TO BE ON THE SAFE SIDE
THE FOLLOWING MORNING.....
BUZZ SNORT BUZZ SNORT BUZZ SNORT
SHUT UP!!
tee tee tee TEE tee tee tee TEE tiddly tiddly TIDDL TEE
CLICK
OOOFFF! SILLY MACHINE!
PIPPAPIPPA PIPPAPIPPA PIPPA PIP PAPIPPA PIPPA PIPPA PIPPA PIPPA
MMMF!! 'STILL TOO EARLY!
MEEP MEEP MEEP MEEP MEEP MEEP MEEP MEEP MEEP
RINGARINGARINGARINGGG!!!
THANK GOODNESS FOR OLD-FASHIONED ALARM CLOCKS!

WHAT AN UNUSUAL-LOOKING PLANT!
IT'S A VENUS FLY-TRAP
A WHAT?
A VENUS FLY-TRAP — IT'S A CARNIVOROUS PLANT. IT EATS INSECTS AND EVEN LITTLE BITS OF MEAT!
UGH! HOW DISGUSTING! A NON-VEGETARIAN PLANT!
WHAT'S DISGUSTING?
WELL, I'M A STRICT VEGETARIAN AND I THINK ITS DISGUSTING TO EAT LIVING THINGS
BUT— PLANTS ARE LIVING THINGS TOO...
DRAT THIS FLY!
BUT THEY DON'T HAVE FEELINGS, THEY DON'T THINK, OR BREATHE— OR AT LEAST NOT IN THE SAME WAY AS US...
ACCORDING TO "THE SECRET LIFE OF PLANTS" THEY FAINT AND GO INTO SHOCK WHEN THEIR LEAVES ARE PLUCKED OR THEIR FLOWERS DESTROYED—
ANYWAY, SHALL WE GO FOR LUNCH?
THERE'S NO POINT FEELING PIOUS ABOUT BEING VEGETARIAN—
SNAP!
—AFTER ALL, FROM THE POINT OF VIEW OF A WHEATFIELD, ALL HUMAN BEINGS ARE
CHEW CHEW CHEW
MASS MURDERERS!
RIGHT ON!
BURP

DID YOU SEE THE REPORT IN LAST WEEK'S NEWSPAPER ABOUT THE NOISE LEVEL IN BOMBAY?
ACCORDING TO W.H.O., THE RECOMMENDED LEVEL OF NOISE IS 45 DECIBELS
THE LEVEL IN BOMBAY, ON AVERAGE, IS 70 DECIBELS
AND DURING FESTIVALS, IT RISES TO 110 DECIBELS!
THAT'S ENOUGH TO DAMAGE ANYONE'S HEARING PERMANENTLY!!
OF COURSE, DURING DIWALI, THE MOST SENSIBLE ACTION TO TAKE IS TO LEAVE TOWN — I WENT TO MATHERAN
DID YOU GO ANYWHERE?
EH?
Manjula

HMMPH!! YOU MODERN WOMEN ARE SO UNROMANTIC!
WHAT'S THE MATTER?
HE CALLED ME UNROMANTIC!
BUT— WHY?
ALL I SAID TO HIM WAS, "I LOVE YOU WITH MY ENTIRE ENDOCRINE SYSTEM!"
UHHH...... I HATE TO SAY THIS BUT I THINK HE WAS RIGHT....
I DON'T! THE ENDOCRINES ARE CRUCIALLY IMPORTANT TO THE BODY'S FUNCTIONS AND... AND...
OK, OK, BUT SOMEHOW, GLANDS AND HORMONES SEEM SO CLINICAL!
CLINICAL?
I MEAN, WHEN YOU'RE IN LOVE YOUR PULSE QUICKENS YOUR THROAT GOES DRY YOU FEEL BREATHLESS-
YEAH..... I THINK I SEE YOUR POINT....
WHAT I SHOULD HAVE SAID WAS, "I LOVE YOU WITH MY ENTIRE CIRCULATORY SYSTEM!" - RIGHT?
Manjula

HE LOVES ME... HE LOVES ME NOT HE LOVES ME HE LOVES ME NOT
HE LOVE'S ME... HE LOVES ME NOT HE LOVES ME.... HE LOVES ME NOT... HE LOVES ME.... HE — OOOOPS!— LOVES ME NOT!!
I'M NOT GOING TO GIVE UP SO EASILY!
HOW ABOUT... HE LIKES ME, HE LIKES ME NOT...
HE LIKES ME... HE LIKES ME NOT... HE LIKES ME.... HE .... OH-OH!
HOWEVER, IT'S STILL NOT CONCLUSIVE!
OKAY, ONE FINAL EFFORT: HE HATES ME.... HE HATES ME NOT.... HE HATES ME....
HE HATES ME NOT... HE HATES ME... HE HATES ME NOT... HE HATES ME... HE HATES ME NOT.. HE HATES ME.... HE HATES ME NOT HE.........
OH DEAR. HE HATES ME!
WELL.
AT LEAST HE'S NOT INDIFFERENT...
Manjula

SUKI?
YES?
OH!
—UH— HI! I'M GLAD TO SEE YOU!
THEY SAY SHE HAS A CRUSH ON ME—
AND WHY'S THAT?
I HAVE SOMETHING IMPORTANT TO SAY TO YOU
AHA! I BET SHE'S GOING TO SAY "I LOVE YOU"!
OH, REALLY?
I'VE BEEN WAITING A LONG TIME TO TELL YOU THIS.....
HEH! HEH! THESE FEMINIST TYPES ARE REAL PUSHOVERS!
LET ME GUESS—IS IT THREE FAMILIAR WORDS?
PRETTY CLOSE! —TWO, ACTUALLY
HUH! SOME VULGAR AMERICANISM, NO DOUBT—
ODD. IT'S USUALLY THREE—
WELL, IF YOU INSIST, I COULD MAKE IT THREE THEN...
WHY SPOIL HER PLEASURE? I'LL LET HER SAY IT!
OKAY, I GIVE UP. WHAT ARE THEY?
MERRY CHRISTMAS, DEEBEE!
Manjula

ISN'T IT A LITTLE LATE FOR NEW YEAR CARDS?
WHY? THERE ARE 358 DAYS TO GO BEFORE IT'S REALLY TOO LATE....
ANYWAY- WHAT I CAME TO ASK ABOUT WAS, WHAT ARRANGEMENTS YOU'VE MADE FOR SEEING THE FILM FESTIVAL
NONE - I'M NOT INTERESTED IN THE STOOPID FESTIVAL!
STRANGE... I THOUGHT YOU LIKED MOVIES
I DO - BUT I ALSO SUFFER FROM A RARE DISEASE CALLED FESTIVALITIS- I HATE GOING TO THESE SOCIETY EVENTS WITH THEIR BORING ART FILMS, THE HUGE CROWDS, THE SILLY CELEBRITIES THE EXORBITANT TICKETS...
WELL. IN THAT CASE, I GUESS I'LL JUST HAVE TO GIVE THIS PASS TO SOMEONE ELSE....
A PASS??
SOME DISEASES ARE EASILY CURED...
SNATCH!

HELLO! WHAT'S GOING ON?
SHH! I'M TRYING TO CONCENTRATE
ON WHAT?
NEVER MIND, YOU WOULDN'T UNDERSTAND!
IT'S YOUR NAVEL, I BET
IT'S THE COSMOS IF YOU MUST KNOW — NOW, WILL YOU LEAVE ME ALONE!
THE COSMOS? WHAT DO YOU KNOW ABOUT THE COSMOS?
STOP TALKING, WILL YOU? YOU'RE DISTURBING ME!
STOP THAT!
BUT I'VE SAID NOTHING AND NO-ONE ASKED YOU TO OPEN YOUR EYES...
YOUR SILENCE DISTURBED ME
OH - ALRIGHT THEN....
?
!
AND NOW, EVEN HIS ABSENCE DISTURBS ME....
Manjula

HI SUKI!
HELLO JANAKI!
WHAT'VE YOU BEEN DOING?
SEEING FILMS AT THE FESTIVAL OF COURSE!
DID YOU SEE WOODY ALLEN'S ZELIG?
YES— I REALLY LOVED THAT ONE—
WHAT WAS IT ABOUT?
WELL, THIS GUY, ZELIG HAD AN AMAZING PROBLEM—HE WOULD BEGIN TO LOOK LIKE ANYONE HE STOOD NEXT TO—EVEN TO THE EXTENT OF CHANGING HIS RACE AND HIS PERSONALITY—
WOULD YOU LIKE TO HAVE SOME COFFEE, BY THE WAY?
A SORT OF HUMAN CHAMELEON?
EXACTLY. IT WAS FUNNY, BUT ALSO QUITE PROFOUND
AFTER ALL IT'S ONLY AN EXAGGERATION OF WHAT HAPPENS TO ALL OF US TO SOME EXTENT
?!
THE MOVIE MUST HAVE LEFT A VERY DEEP IMPRESSION ON YOU—
WHAT MAKES YOU SAY THAT, I WONDER?

AND NOW, I'M GOING TO CLEAR MY MIND OF ALL THOUGHT AND CONCENTRATE ON SILENCE
SILENCE.
SILENCE. SILENCE. SILENCE. SILENCE. SILENCE. SILENCE.
SILENCE. SILENCE! SIL ENCE! SILE
SILENCE! SILENCE! SILENCE! SILENCE! SILENCE!
POP!
PHEW!
THAT WAS A TRULY EAR-SPLITTING SILENCE!
Manjula

WHAT GOT YOU INTERESTED IN MEDITATION?
I READ A BOOK WHICH SAID THAT ONE COULD GAIN DIVINE POWERS THROUGH MEDITATION
WELL, IT LOOKS LIKE YOU SUCCEEDED HUH?
YOU MEAN FROM MY AURA OF SANCTITY?
WELL-
OR MY AIR OF BLISSFUL SERENITY?
NO, NOT QUITE
THE GENTLE BUDDHA-LIKE SMILE ON MY FACE, THEN?
NO, NOT THAT EITHER
OR THE MYSTIC EXPRESSION IN MY HALF-SHUT EYES?
NO, IT'S SOMETHING A LITTLE MORE...
..OBVIOUS...

DOESN'T IT FEEL ODD TO HAVE FOUR ARMS?
ACTUALLY, THEY'RE QUITE USEFUL...
FOR PLAYING TWO HANDS OF RUMMY SIMULTANEOUSLY F'R INSTANCE
...AND THEY'RE GREAT FOR PUTTING CURLERS IN ONE'S HAIR...
...IDEAL FOR MOUNTAINEERING
...INDISPENSABLE FOR EATING CHICKEN AT A BUFFET...
...AND FOR STANDING STEADY IN A B.E.S.T. BUS....
!
...IN FACT, THE ONLY REAL DRAWBACK IS THAT...
...MY TAILORING COSTS HAVE DOUBLED...
Manjula

WHAT ARE YOU MEDITATING ABOUT NOW?
WORLD PEACE -IN A MANNER OF SPEAKING....
WHAT DO YOU MEAN?
WELL- I'VE DECIDED I DON'T WANT THIS EXTRA PAIR OF LIMBS ANY MORE....
OKAY -AND SO?
SO — I'M MEDITATING TO MAKE THEM GO AWAY AGAIN
BUT WHAT DOES THAT HAVE TO DO WITH WORLD PEACE?
WOULDN'T YOU CALL THIS VOLUNTARY BILATERAL DISARMAMENT?

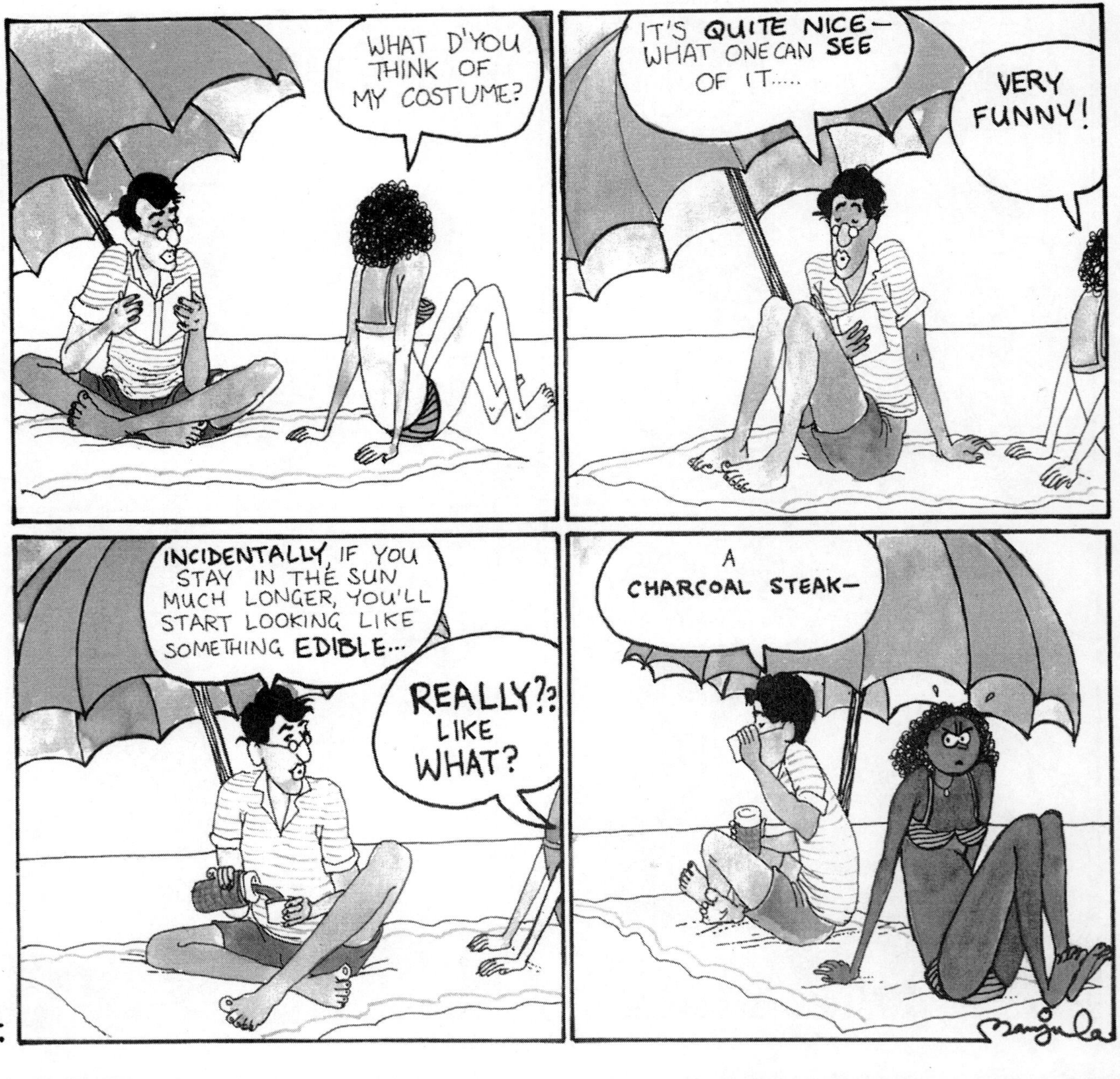
WHAT D'YOU THINK OF MY COSTUME?
IT'S QUITE NICE— WHAT ONE CAN SEE OF IT.....
VERY FUNNY!
INCIDENTALLY, IF YOU STAY IN THE SUN MUCH LONGER, YOU'LL START LOOKING LIKE SOMETHING EDIBLE...
REALLY?? LIKE WHAT?
A CHARCOAL STEAK—
Manjula

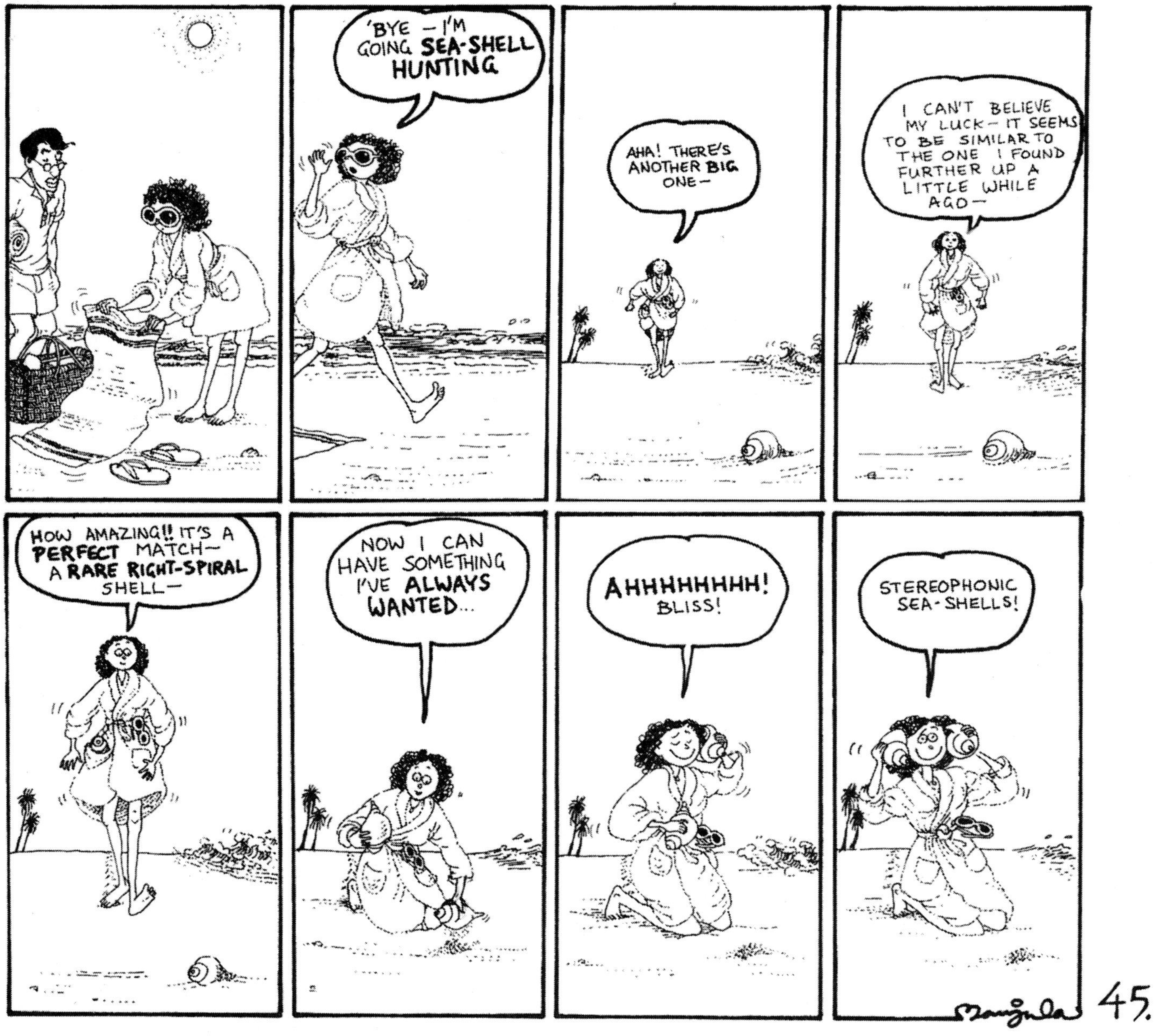

'BYE — I'M GOING SEA-SHELL HUNTING
AHA! THERE'S ANOTHER BIG ONE—
I CAN'T BELIEVE MY LUCK— IT SEEMS TO BE SIMILAR TO THE ONE I FOUND FURTHER UP A LITTLE WHILE AGO—
HOW AMAZING!! IT'S A PERFECT MATCH— A RARE RIGHT-SPIRAL SHELL—
NOW I CAN HAVE SOMETHING I'VE ALWAYS WANTED...
AHHHHHHHH! BLISS!
STEREOPHONIC SEA-SHELLS!
Manjula

THERE'S NO SOUND MORE RELAXING THAN THE MURMURING OF A SEA-SHELL...
LIKE HOLDING THE OCEANS' VOICE TO ONE'S EAR... WHO KNOWS WHAT COSMIC SECRETS ONE MIGHT STUMBLE ACROSS?
I COULD SIT HERE FOREVER EAVESDROPPING AT NATURE'S KEYHOLE LISTENING TO THIS ETERNAL WHISPERING...
MURMURMURM
MURMURMURMURMUR
IT'S LATE FOR LUNCH DUMMY! AND THE SANDWICHES ARE ALL STALE AND THE COFFEE'S GONE COLD... SO GET BACK AT ONCE!
"IT'S LATE FOR LUNCH, DUMMY!" IS A COSMIC SECRET??
I MUST HAVE HEARD WRONG...
IN THE FACE OF INFINITY, WHAT IS THE MEANING OF LUNCH??!

YOU USED TO HAVE NIGHTMARES ABOUT BULLS RIGHT?
YES! TERRIBLE ONES!
HMM! INTERESTING.
THEY WERE MY WORST AND MOST FRIGHTENING NIGHTMARES!
WHAT WERE THEY LIKE?
I USED TO DREAM I WAS BEING CHASED BY A HUGE BLACK BULL, LIKE THE ONES IN SPANISH BULLFIGHTS..
AND HAS ANYTHING LIKE THAT EVER HAPPENED TO YOU?
NO NEVER, THANK GOD! I DON'T THINK I'D SURVIVE IT!
AND WHAT HAPPENED TO THE NIGHTMARES?
I WENT TO A PSYCHIATRIST WHO CONVINCED ME THAT MY FEARS WERE BASELESS
ANYWAY - WHY D'YOU WANT TO KNOW
WELL... I JUST WANTED TO BE SURE...
AAARGH! THE BULL!!!
THAT AT LAST YOU WERE GOING TO SEE...
... A DREAM COME TRUE!

HI! I HEARD YOU WERE IN HOSPITAL
YEAH — I HAD AN ENCOUNTER WITH A BIG BLACK BULL!
WOW! THAT MUST HAVE BEEN AWFUL! WHAT HAPPENED??
WELL.... I WAS TOSSED 20 FEET IN THE AIR, AND LANDED ON A FIRE HYDRANT
I BROKE BOTH MY ARMS, WAS GORED IN THE STOMACH AND HAVE MULTIPLE RIB FRACTURES...
....AND MAY NEVER WALK PROPERLY AGAIN!!
GEE, THAT'S REALLY SAD — BUT WHAT I MEANT WAS, WHAT HAPPENED TO THE BULL?
manjula

YOU REMEMBER, DR. SCHRINCK, MY NIGHTMARES ABOUT BEING CHASED BY BULLS?
...AND YOU SHOWED ME HOW SILLY MY FEARS WERE? REMEMBER?
WELL, YOU WERE WRONG!!!
A COUPLE OF WEEKS AGO, I WAS REALLY CHASED BY A HUGE BLACK BULL AND IT WAS TERRIBLE, WORSE THAN ANY DREAM....
NOW I'LL NEVER BE ABLE TO TRUST ANYONE AGAIN....
...AND THE NIGHTMARES HAVE STARTED AGAIN....
....EXCEPT, NOW IT'S NOT JUST ONE BULL BUT A WHOLE HERD!
BIG ONES, SMALL ONES, ALL KINDS OF BREEDS... JERSEYS, BRAHMINIS, HOLSTEINS, FRIESIANS YORKSHIRES, RED SINDHIS, EVEN A COUPLE OF BUFFALOES!
I CAN'T SLEEP A WINK!!!
OOOOHHH!! DOCTOR, TELL ME WHAT TO DO!
HAVE YOU CONSIDERED BECOMING A VET?

HEY!
HEY, PRINCESS!
DID I HEAR SOMEONE SAY "HEY, PRINCESS"?
YEAH- I DID, DOWN HERE!
IT'S — IT'S — A TALKING FROG!
NOT JUST ANY TALKING FROG! — I'M A FROG PRINCE!!
WANNA KISS??
YECH!! WHO'D WANT TO KISS A FROG, PRINCE OR NO PRINCE?
BUT- IT'S LIKE THE FAIRYTALE - REMEMBER? THE PRINCESS KISSES THE FROG AND BREAKS THE EVIL SPELL AND HE BECOMES A HANDSOME PRINCE, AGAIN?
HOW DO I KNOW YOU'RE NOT MAKING A FOOL OF ME, JUST TO GET A FREE KISS?
LOOK! HERE'S THE CONTRACT WITH THE TERMS AND CONDITIONS OF THE EVIL SPELL!
"THIS BLAHBLAHBLAH HEREBY CERTIFIES BLAHBLAHBLAHBLAH THAT PRINCE BLAH BLAHBLAH WAS SUMMARILY BLAHBLAH ENCHANTED BLAHBLAHBLAH BLAH AND CAN ONLY BE BLAHBL RELEASED BLAHBLAHBLAHBLAH BLAH BY A KISS BLAHBLAH BLAHBLAHBLAHBLAH BLAH
OH PLEASE! PLEASE, PLEASE, PLEASE, PLEASE, PLEASE, PLEASE PLEASE! DO ME THIS TINY FAVOR!
OH ALRIGHT, THEN! -IF IT MEANS SO MUCH TO YOU-
PLOCH!
RRIP!
......AND WHAT MAKES YOU THINK YOU'RE A PRINCESS??

I HOPE MY LITTLE DECEPTION HASN'T PUT YOU OFF ME FOREVER?
JUST BECAUSE I'M NOT A FROG PRINCE...
DOESN'T MEAN...
THAT WE CAN'T HAVE.....
...A DEEP AND MEANINGFUL RELATIONSHIP, RIGHT?
WELL... I THINK THERE IS ONE IMMEDIATE PRACTICAL PROBLEM TO BE SOLVED...
YOU MEAN, THAT I'M A FROG AND YOU'RE A HUMAN?
NO-
THAT YOU CAN'T SWIM UNDERWATER?
NO-
THAT YOUR PARENTS MIGHT OBJECT?
NO-
THEN WHAT?
I CAN'T UNCROSS MY EYES...
Manjula

YOU LIKE SITTING THERE ON MY HEAD, HUH?
YEAH - IT REALLY GETS ME HIGH!!
'CEPT FOR ONE SMALL PROBLEM-
AH—
-AH-
-AH-
-AH-
AH-
TISHOO!
ARE YOU OKAY? HAVE YOU CAUGHT A COLD?
NO—
-I'M ALLERGIC TO DANDRUFF...
Manjula

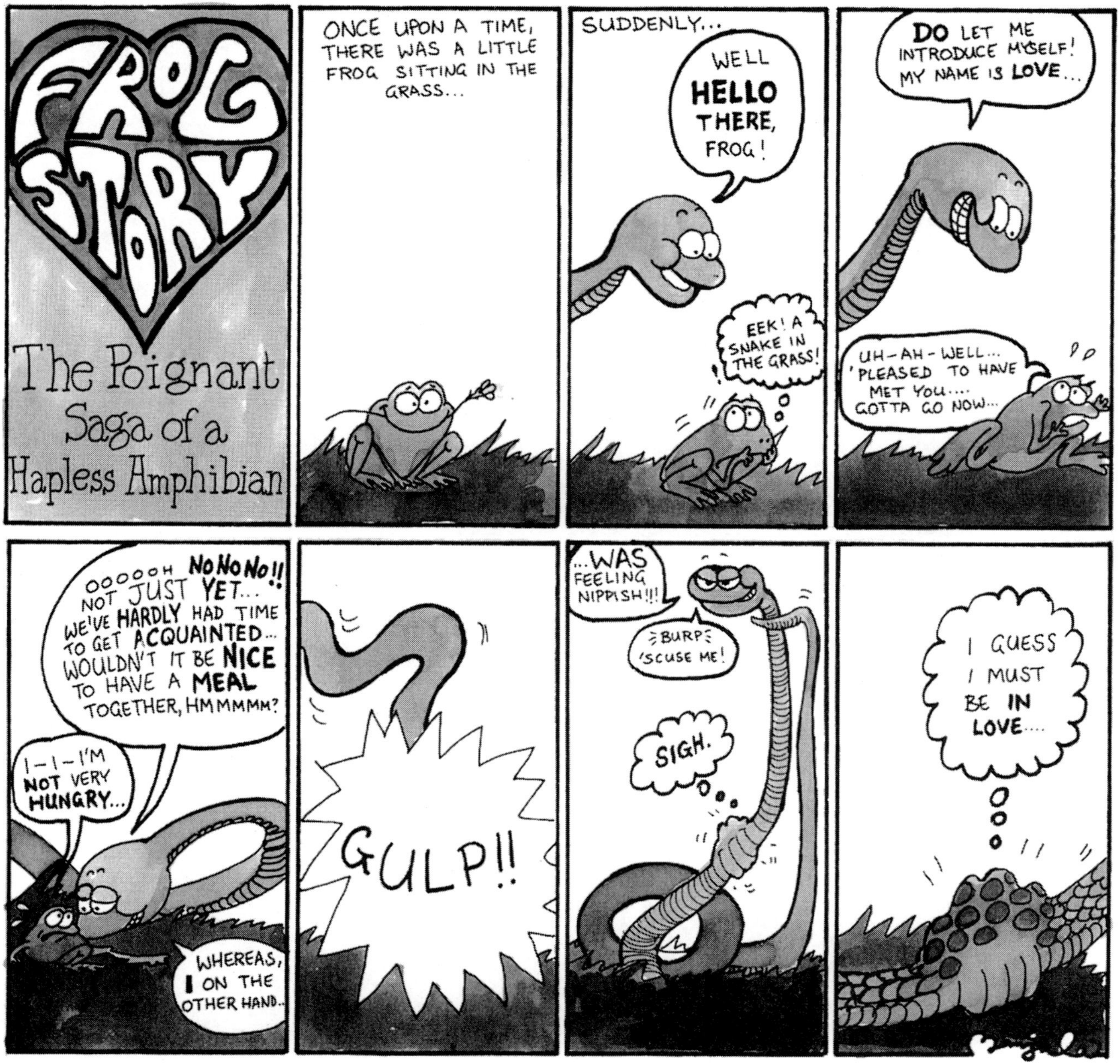
FROG STORY
The Poignant Saga of a Hapless Amphibian
ONCE UPON A TIME, THERE WAS A LITTLE FROG SITTING IN THE GRASS...
SUDDENLY...
WELL HELLO THERE, FROG!
EEK! A SNAKE IN THE GRASS!
DO LET ME INTRODUCE MYSELF! MY NAME IS LOVE...
UH-AH-WELL... PLEASED TO HAVE MET YOU.... GOTTA GO NOW...
OOOOOOH NO NO NO!! NOT JUST YET... WE'VE HARDLY HAD TIME TO GET ACQUAINTED... WOULDN'T IT BE NICE TO HAVE A MEAL TOGETHER, HMMMMM?
I-I-I'M NOT VERY HUNGRY...
WHEREAS, I ON THE OTHER HAND...
GULP!!
...WAS FEELING NIPPISH!!!
BURP 'SCUSE ME!
SIGH.
I GUESS I MUST BE IN LOVE....

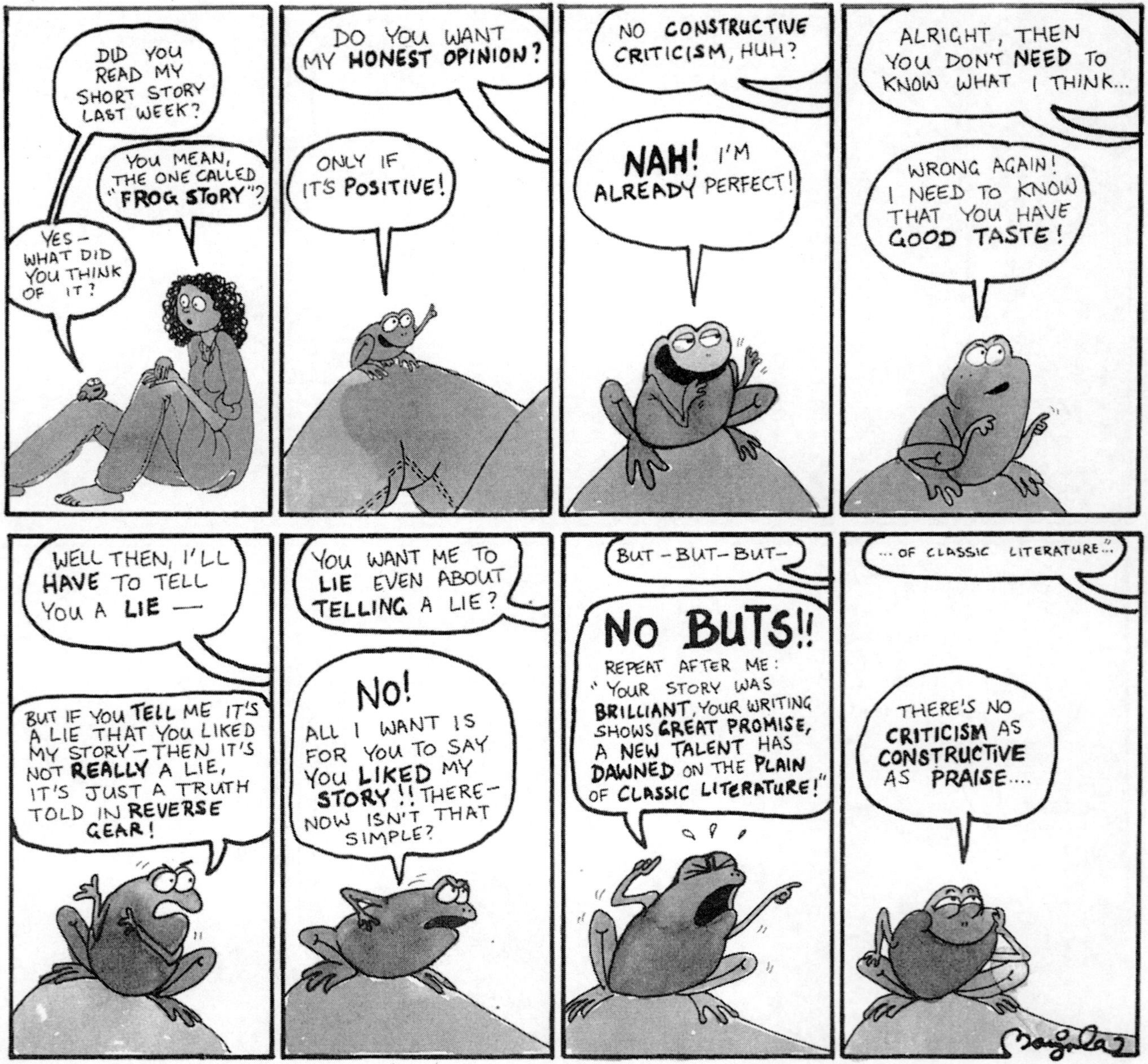
DID YOU READ MY SHORT STORY LAST WEEK?
YOU MEAN, THE ONE CALLED "FROG STORY"?
YES — WHAT DID YOU THINK OF IT?
DO YOU WANT MY HONEST OPINION?
ONLY IF IT'S POSITIVE!
NO CONSTRUCTIVE CRITICISM, HUH?
NAH! I'M ALREADY PERFECT!
ALRIGHT, THEN YOU DON'T NEED TO KNOW WHAT I THINK...
WRONG AGAIN! I NEED TO KNOW THAT YOU HAVE GOOD TASTE!
WELL THEN, I'LL HAVE TO TELL YOU A LIE —
BUT IF YOU TELL ME IT'S A LIE THAT YOU LIKED MY STORY — THEN IT'S NOT REALLY A LIE, IT'S JUST A TRUTH TOLD IN REVERSE GEAR!
YOU WANT ME TO LIE EVEN ABOUT TELLING A LIE?
NO! ALL I WANT IS FOR YOU TO SAY YOU LIKED MY STORY!! THERE — NOW ISN'T THAT SIMPLE?
BUT — BUT — BUT —
NO BUTS!! REPEAT AFTER ME: "YOUR STORY WAS BRILLIANT, YOUR WRITING SHOWS GREAT PROMISE, A NEW TALENT HAS DAWNED ON THE PLAIN OF CLASSIC LITERATURE!"
... OF CLASSIC LITERATURE..."
THERE'S NO CRITICISM AS CONSTRUCTIVE AS PRAISE....
Bouzola

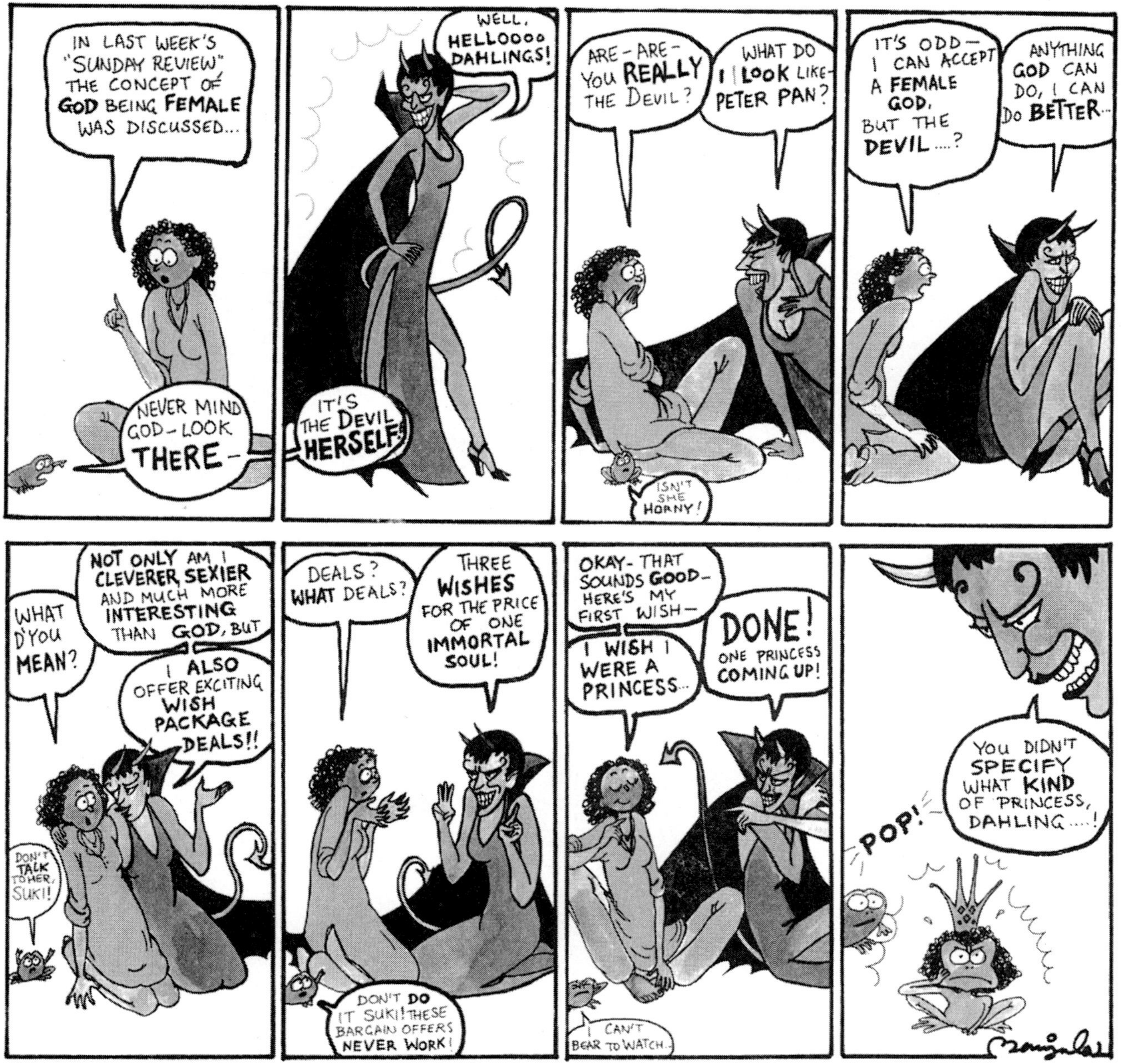
IN LAST WEEK'S "SUNDAY REVIEW" THE CONCEPT OF GOD BEING FEMALE WAS DISCUSSED...
NEVER MIND GOD - LOOK THERE -
WELL, HELLOOOO DAHLINGS!
IT'S THE DEVIL HERSELF!
ARE - ARE - YOU REALLY THE DEVIL?
WHAT DO I LOOK LIKE - PETER PAN?
ISN'T SHE HORNY!
IT'S ODD - I CAN ACCEPT A FEMALE GOD, BUT THE DEVIL....?
ANYTHING GOD CAN DO, I CAN DO BETTER...
WHAT D'YOU MEAN?
NOT ONLY AM I CLEVERER, SEXIER AND MUCH MORE INTERESTING THAN GOD, BUT
I ALSO OFFER EXCITING WISH PACKAGE DEALS!!
DON'T TALK TO HER, SUKI!
DEALS? WHAT DEALS?
THREE WISHES FOR THE PRICE OF ONE IMMORTAL SOUL!
DON'T DO IT SUKI! THESE BARGAIN OFFERS NEVER WORK!
OKAY - THAT SOUNDS GOOD - HERE'S MY FIRST WISH -
I WISH I WERE A PRINCESS...
DONE! ONE PRINCESS COMING UP!
I CAN'T BEAR TO WATCH...
POP!
YOU DIDN'T SPECIFY WHAT KIND OF PRINCESS, DAHLING....!
Manjula

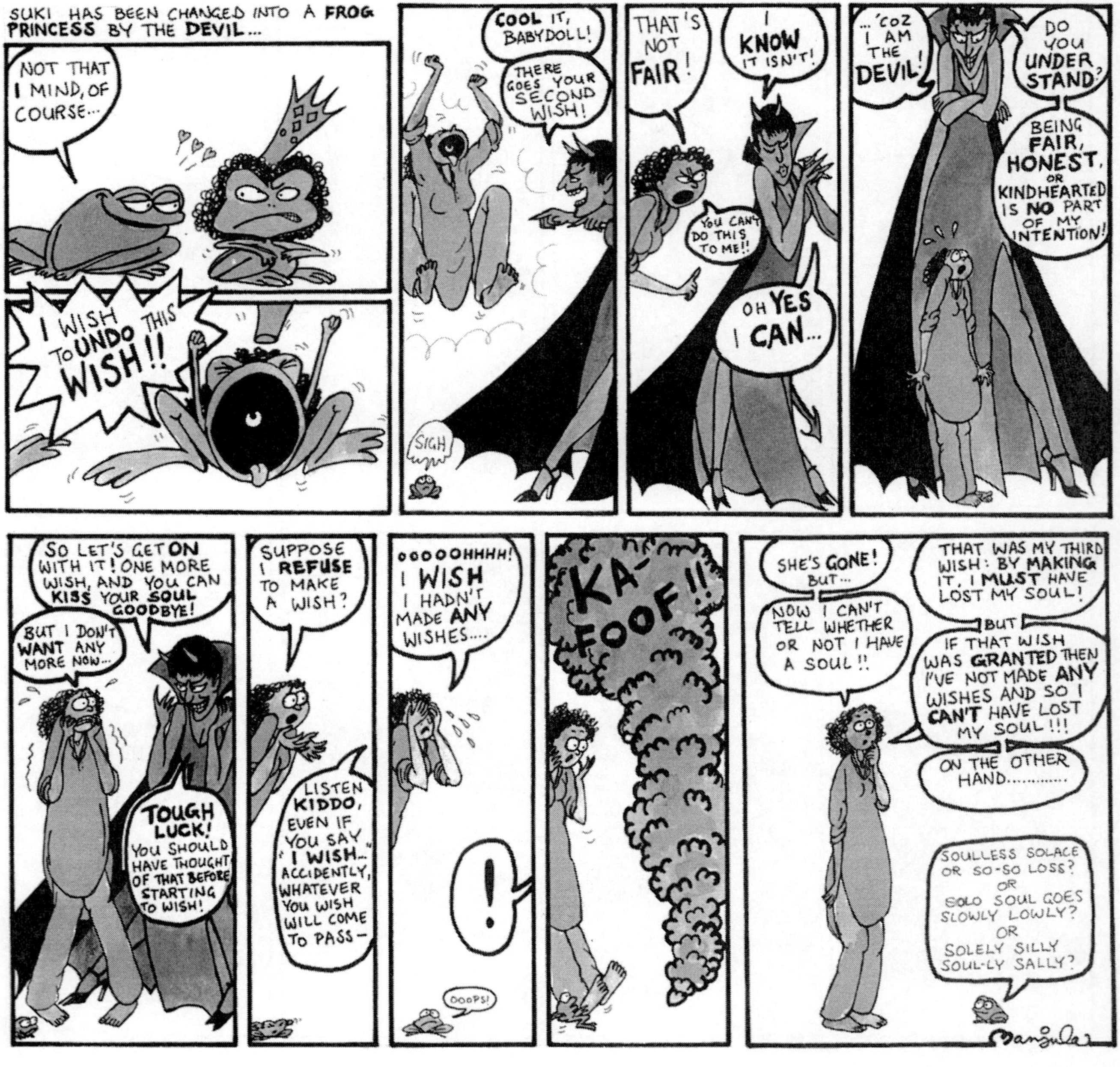
SUKI HAS BEEN CHANGED INTO A FROG PRINCESS BY THE DEVIL...
NOT THAT I MIND, OF COURSE...
I WISH TO UNDO THIS WISH!!
COOL IT, BABYDOLL!
THERE GOES YOUR SECOND WISH!
SIGH
THAT'S NOT FAIR!
I KNOW IT ISN'T!
YOU CAN'T DO THIS TO ME!!
OH YES I CAN...
...'COZ I AM THE DEVIL!
DO YOU UNDERSTAND?
BEING FAIR, HONEST, OR KINDHEARTED IS NO PART OF MY INTENTION!
SO LET'S GET ON WITH IT! ONE MORE WISH, AND YOU CAN KISS YOUR SOUL GOODBYE!
BUT I DON'T WANT ANY MORE NOW...
TOUGH LUCK! YOU SHOULD HAVE THOUGHT OF THAT BEFORE STARTING TO WISH!
SUPPOSE I REFUSE TO MAKE A WISH?
LISTEN KIDDO, EVEN IF YOU SAY "I WISH..." ACCIDENTLY, WHATEVER YOU WISH WILL COME TO PASS—
OOOOOHHHH! I WISH I HADN'T MADE ANY WISHES....
!
OOOPS!
KA-FOOF!!
SHE'S GONE! BUT...
NOW I CAN'T TELL WHETHER OR NOT I HAVE A SOUL!!
THAT WAS MY THIRD WISH: BY MAKING IT, I MUST HAVE LOST MY SOUL!
BUT
IF THAT WISH WAS GRANTED THEN I'VE NOT MADE ANY WISHES AND SO I CAN'T HAVE LOST MY SOUL!!!
ON THE OTHER HAND............
SOULLESS SOLACE OR SO-SO LOSS? OR SOLO SOUL GOES SLOWLY LOWLY? OR SOLELY SILLY SOUL-LY SALLY?
Manjula

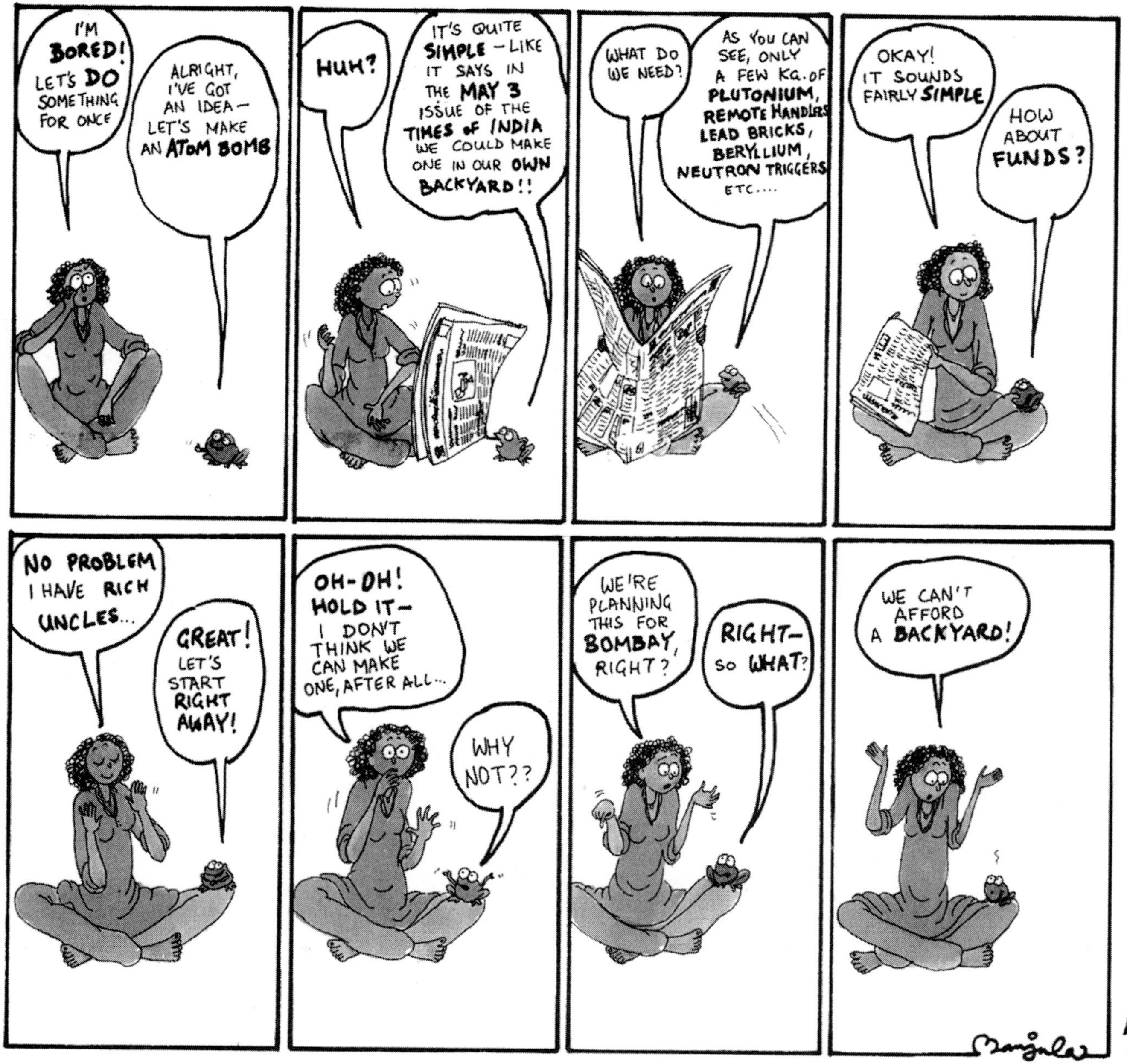
I'M BORED! LET'S DO SOMETHING FOR ONCE
ALRIGHT, I'VE GOT AN IDEA— LET'S MAKE AN ATOM BOMB
HUH?
IT'S QUITE SIMPLE — LIKE IT SAYS IN THE MAY 3 ISSUE OF THE TIMES OF INDIA WE COULD MAKE ONE IN OUR OWN BACKYARD!!
WHAT DO WE NEED?
AS YOU CAN SEE, ONLY A FEW Kg. OF PLUTONIUM, REMOTE HANDLERS LEAD BRICKS, BERYLLIUM, NEUTRON TRIGGERS ETC....
OKAY! IT SOUNDS FAIRLY SIMPLE
HOW ABOUT FUNDS?
NO PROBLEM I HAVE RICH UNCLES...
GREAT! LET'S START RIGHT AWAY!
OH-OH! HOLD IT— I DON'T THINK WE CAN MAKE ONE, AFTER ALL...
WHY NOT??
WE'RE PLANNING THIS FOR BOMBAY, RIGHT?
RIGHT— SO WHAT?
WE CAN'T AFFORD A BACKYARD!
Manjula

OH-OH! IT'S STARTING TO RAIN...
IT'S A GOOD THING I REMEMBERED MY UMBRELLA - OOOPS!
FRIP!
- IF I CAN GET IT TO WORK, THAT IS!
THERE- OOOPS!
GRRRRR! THIS IS STARTING TO BUG ME!
HERE WE GO- AHA! MADE IT —
HEY-!!
WELL... I GUESS... IT'S BETTER THAN LEAVING IT BEHIND IN THE BUS....

THE DREAM
PRODUCED BY: SUKI
DIRECTED BY: S. UKI
PHOTOGRAPHED BY: S.U. KI
STARRING: SU KI
STARRING SU KI
ZZZZ....OOOH. I'M AWAKE!
IT'S SIX O'CLOCK IN THE MORNING.....
AND I FEEL WONDERFUL!!
I JUST LOVE TO WAKE UP!!
I'M SO THRILLED TO BE AWAKE!!
POP!
HEY! WAKE UP! IT'S TEN O'CLOCK!!
WHA'- WHO- HUH?~ !!
GO 'WAY! LEAVE ME ALONE!! I WAS HAVING A NICE DREAM!
WHAT WAS IT ABOUT?
I DREAMT I WAS GLAD TO BE AWAKE!
ALL RIGHT- SO WAKE UP AND BE GLAD!
NO! I HAVE TO GET BACK INTO THE DREAM
WHY?
TO FIND OUT WHAT I WAS GLAD ABOUT....
Manjula

HMMM! I WONDER WHAT THIS BUMP IS?
WHAT BUMP?
AAAARGH! NOW IT'S A DEPRESSION!
NO, NOW IT'S A BUMP!
ANOTHER BUMP! IT MUST BE AN EARTHQUAKE
MEANWHILE I'M BACK IN THE PITS!
PHEW! I'M GLAD THAT'S OVER
DON'T SPEAK TOO SOON
SEE WHAT I MEAN?
OOOPS! HERE WE GO AGAIN! WHAT IS ALL THIS?
RANDOM PIECES IN THE PUZZLE OF EXISTENCE, PERHAPS?
Manjula

AAAARGH!!
A-A-A-
COCKROACH!!
OOOOOOOOOH! PLEASEPLEASEPLEASE GET RID OF IT FOR ME!
HMMPH! YOU WOMEN MAKE SUCH A FUSS ABOUT THESE LITTLE THINGS!
YEEEESH!
ALL YOU HAVE TO DO IS KILL THEM- YAH! LIKE THIS-
SPLAT!
SEE? JUST A LITTLE BLOOD AND GORE-
YUCK! C'MON, LET'S GET AWAY FROM THIS CARNAGE-
GOOD IDEA! ALL THIS PEST CONTROL HAS GIVEN ME AN APPETITE...
ONE DOWN...
9,999,999,999 TO GO!

I HEAR YOU'RE ON A DIET?
YES— FOR TWO DAYS ONLY APPLES
YUCK! DON'T YOU GET TIRED OF THEM?
WELL, I LIKE APPLES!
RUMBLE!
DO I HEAR THUNDER
HMMM! I THINK THAT WAS MY STOMACH!
GROWL!
PERHAPS YOU'RE HUNGRY?
BUT I DON'T FEEL HUNGRY! I'VE JUST EATEN FOUR APPLES!
ROAR! SNARL!
SQUEAK!
LOOKS LIKE YOUR STOMACH DOESN'T AGREE!
QUIET, YOU! YOU'RE FULL, SO PIPE DOWN!
GROAN!
MMOAN
JUST A LITTLE SNACK PERHAPS?
I'M NOT HUNGRY!
YOWL!
SCREAM!
!
I'M NOT HUNGRY. I'M NOT HUNGRY, I'M NOT HUNGRY...
OW! OW! OW!
ARROOOO
ROWFF!
GRROO OOOO
WHINE!
STOMACHS SPEAK LOUDER THAN WORDS.....
Manjula

MY STOMACH AND I HAVE ENTERED A NEW ERA OF COOPERATION!
I WON'T GO ON CRASH DIETS —
AND IT WILL ADVISE ME ON WHAT'S BEST FOR OUR BODY'S NEEDS...
FROM NOW ON IT'S GOING TO BE SALADS ALL THE WAY! NO SWEETS, NO FRIED THINGS, NO STARCHY THINGS, NO—
SNORT!
WHAT'S THAT? BROWNIES ARE VITAL FOR NUTRITION?
ALL RIGHT, THEN — — WHAT? BUTTER TOO? WELL.... IF YOU SAY SO...
YOU'RE SURE? KAJU BARFI IS SLIMMING? BIRYANI TOO? — WHAT?— YOU GIVE ME YOUR WORD? GHEE, HUH?
LATER, MUCH LATER,
... NEVER TRUST A HUNGRY STOMACH!
URP!
Manjula

ACTUALLY,
BEING ENORMOUSLY FAT IS NOT AS TERRIBLE AS IT'S MADE OUT TO BE ....
F'RINSTANCE, ONE IS AT PEACE WITH ONE'S STOMACH
NO MORE AGONY AT MEALTIMES NO MORE BATTLES WITH BULGES NO MORE SWEETEX NO MORE CELERY.... LIFE BECOMES ONE LONG, GORGING FEAST!
NO MORE JANE FONDA'S WORKOUTS! NO MORE EXERCYCLES! NO MORE ISOMETRICS! NO MORE AEROBICS! NO MORE CALISTHENICS! NO...
HIYA FATSO!
....NO MORE FRIENDS....

SUKI! WHAT'S HAPPENED! WHY ARE YOU LYING SO STILL???
IT'S TOO MUCH EFFORT TO SIT UP
BUT ARE YOU ALL RIGHT??
FINE!
YOU DON'T LOOK FINE....
A TEENY BIT OVERWEIGHT, PERHAPS?
A "TEENY BIT"??? YOU LOOK LIKE A BEACHED WHALE!!
SURELY YOU EXAGGERATE?
LISTEN- I KNOW I SHOULDN'T INTERFERE BUT I FEEL I MUST GIVE YOU SOME ADVISE...
YES?
I THINK YOU SHOULD STOP YOUR UNCONTROLLED EATING...
ALL RIGHT.
WELL! THAT WAS QUICK! I THOUGHT YOU'D SHOW MORE RESISTANCE!
NO. WHY?
IT'S TOO MUCH EFFORT TO EAT

WELL?
WHAT **EXERCISES** ARE YOU DOING TO **LOSE WEIGHT**?
CAN'T YOU **SEE**?
Manjula

WELL?? HOW DO I LOOK?
LIKE A PREGNANT ZEBRA
REALLY? I THOUGHT VERTICAL STRIPES WOULD BE SLIMMING...
NO, THE CAFTAN IS TOO WIDE AND TENT-LIKE TO BE SLIMMING
HOW ABOUT THIS, THEN?
UGH! THE BEACH BALL EFFECT!
AND NOW?
THE ARMOURED TANK EFFECT—
CAN'T YOU SAY ANYTHING ENCOURAGING?
SURE!
YOU'RE THE CUTEST ARMOURED TANK I EVER MET!!

OH!
YOU GAVE ME A FRIGHT! -AND WHO ARE YOU, ANYWAY?
I AM THE POET
WHAT D'YOU MEAN, THE POET?
I WRITE POETRY....
REALLY?? WILL YOU RECITE SOME FOR ME?
SURE.
AHEM
BUT... BUT.... I CAN'T HEAR ANYTHING!!
WELL NATURALLY- YOU CAN'T!
IT'S BLANK VERSE —
Manjula

MY NEW POEM IS ENTITLED "DEAFENED HILLS" HERE'S THE FIRST VERSE:
"I WANDERED, LONELY AS A CLOWN THAT DRIFTS ON LOWS AND FLOATS ON HIGHS
'TILL ALL AT ONCE I SAW SOME BROWN AND POLKA-DOTTED SPANISH FLIES" —
WELL?? WHAT D'YOU THINK SO FAR
IT SOUNDS EXTREMELY FAMILIAR!
LIKE ANOTHER POEM, YOU MEAN?
A VERY WELL-KNOWN ONE, CALLED "DAFFODILS" EVERY SCHOOL CHILD KNOWS IT, IT'S THAT WELL-KNOWN!
ODD! I'VE NEVER HEARD OF IT!
HOW IGNORANT, UNINFORMED AND DULL CAN YOU BE? NEXT YOU'LL SAY YOU DON'T KNOW WHO WROTE IT!!
I DON'T — WHO WAS IT?
SHAKESPEARE, OF COURSE!!
Manjula

HEY!
!
WHAT'RE YOU DOING ON THE CEILING??
COME DOWN AT ONCE!
BUT-BUT, I'M NOT ON THE CEILING, YOU ARE!
NONSENSE! ANY FOOL KNOWS UP FROM DOWN AND YOU'RE UP!!
WELL THERE'S ONLY ONE WAY OF PROVING IT —
WHAT'S THAT?
WHEN THAT SIGNATURE APPEARS IN THAT CORNER, YOU'LL SEE THAT I'M RIGHT
WHAT SIGNATURE?
OH....NEVER MIND —

I CAN'T GET OVER THE FEELING THAT I'M THE WRONG WAY UP-
I CAN'T THINK WHY!
LOOK AT THE REST OF THIS NEWSPAPER-
IT'S JUST A PRINTING ERROR!
STILL— I'D RATHER CHECK WITH THE READERS-
WHO, THEM? OUT THERE, READING THIS COMIC STRIP??
WELL, THEY'D KNOW FOR SURE-
WHY? THEY'RE AS CONFUSED AS YOU ARE—
HOW D'YOU KNOW
THEY'RE THE ONES HOLDING THEIR NEWSPAPERS UPSIDE DOWN!

HAVE YOU SEEN SUKI ANYWHERE?
YES....
... SHE'S SLEEPING....
HOW PEACEFUL SHE LOOKS!
YEH-
- JUST LIKE THE FAIRYTALE...
FAIRYTALE? WHICH FAIRYTALE??
"SLEEPING UGLY"!
Manjula

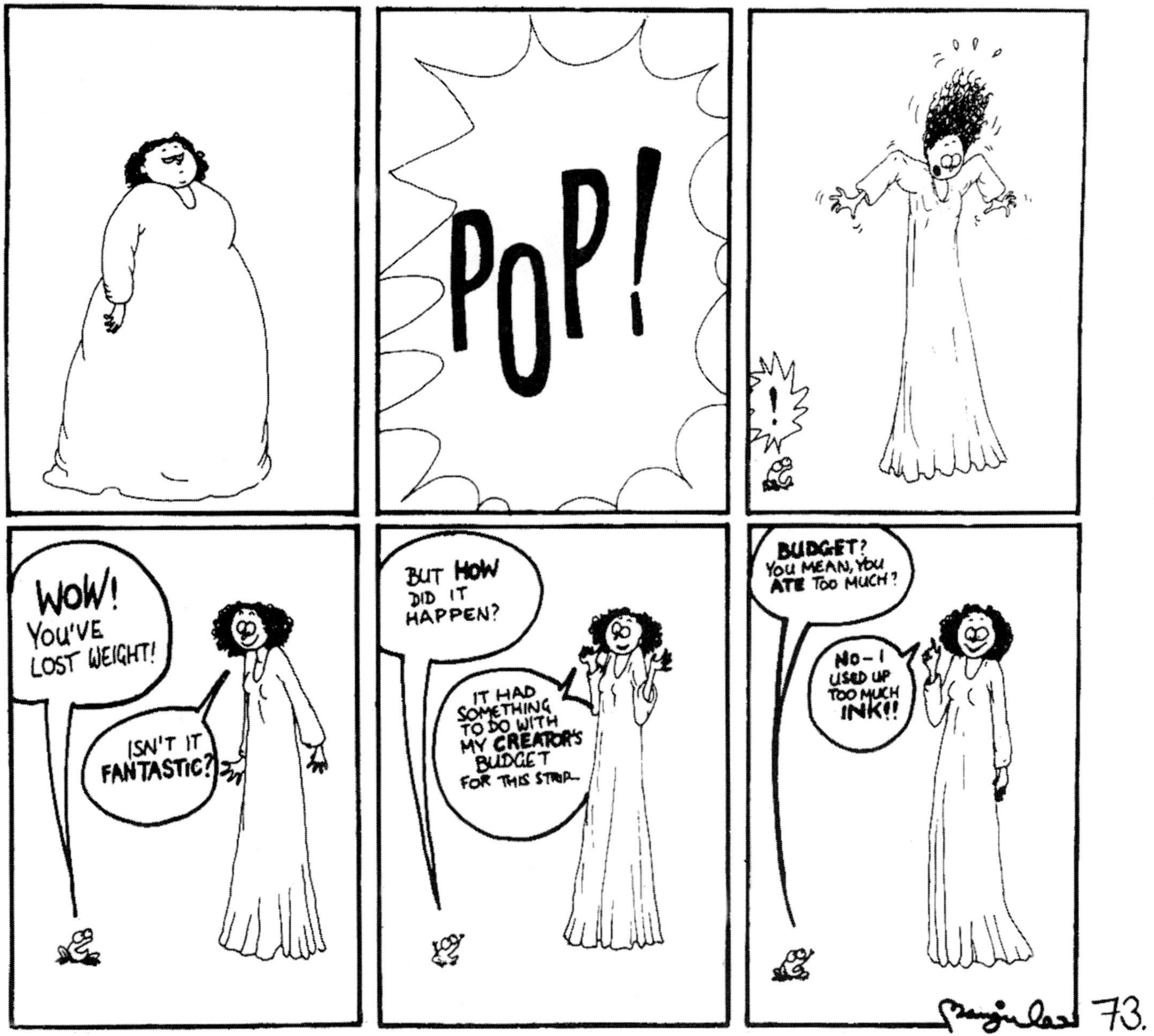
POP!
!
WOW! YOU'VE LOST WEIGHT!
ISN'T IT FANTASTIC?
BUT HOW DID IT HAPPEN?
IT HAD SOMETHING TO DO WITH MY CREATOR'S BUDGET FOR THIS STRIP.
BUDGET? YOU MEAN, YOU ATE TOO MUCH?
NO – I USED UP TOO MUCH INK!!

DO YOU BELIEVE IN ASTROLOGY?
SORT OF— WHY?
WHAT IS YOUR STAR-SIGN?
TAKE A GUESS—
AQUARIUS? VIRGO? SCORPIO?
NO— NO— NO—
I GIVE UP! WHAT ARE YOU?
A PISCEAN!
REALLY?!
AND WHAT ARE YOU?
A LEO!
AND WHAT ARE YOU?
A FROG!

THIS IS AGENT BEEP REPORTING FROM PLANET S3
I SHALL NOW PROCEED ON MY SECRET MISSION....
AHA! TWO UNIDENTIFIED LIFE FORMS APPROACHING!
I'LL MAKE MYSELF INVISIBLE IN ORDER TO OBSERVE THEM UNAWARES—
POP!
SUKI?
YES?
HMMM!
WHAT KIND OF POP MUSIC DO YOU LIKE BEST?
THE BEATLES, FIRST AND FOREVER!
— THEN THE DOORS
—THEN THE STONES
— THEN PINK FLOYD
—THEN THE WHO...
—THEN SOME PUNK
—THEN DAVID BOWIE
INTERESTING!! VERY INTERESTING!!!
POP
PERSONALLY, I PREFER BACH —
Manjula

I MUST MAKE CONTACT WITH THE NATIVES OF THIS PLANET
BUT FIRST— MY DISGUISE....
THEN – MY PHRASE BOOK.
HMMMMM..... ..."COMMON WORDS AND PHRASES".....
AHA! THERE'S AN EARTHLING!
AHEM!
"WHAT'S NEW, PUSSYCAT?"
EEEEEK! A MARTIAN!!
DRAT! SHE RECOGNIZED THE ACCENT....

HOW INTERESTING! A BI-LINGUAL ECHO POINT!
IMAGINE!
BI-LINGUAL ECHO POINT ENGLISH/FRENCH
WHAT SHALL I CALL OUT?
HOW ABOUT "YOOHOO"?
OKAY! YOOHOO!
WHO? WHO? WHO? WHO? WHO? WHO WHO?
THERE'S THE ENGLISH—
IT'S ASKING YOU WHO YOU ARE!
WHO? WHO? WHO? WHO? WHO?
BUT— WHERE'S THE FRENCH?
ANSWER THE QUESTION!
WHAT QUESTION?
WHO? WHO? WHO? WHO! WHO? WHO?
TELL THE ECHO WHO YOU ARE—
OKAY— I'M SUKI!
QUI? QUI? QUI? QUI? QUI? QUI? QUI?
—AND THERE'S THE FRENCH!

I TOOK YOUR ADVISE AND GOT MYSELF A PET!!
HMM! SO I SEE
ISN'T HE CUTE?
FOR A RAT, VERY
HE'S NOT A RAT!!
NO?
HE'S A CHIHUAHUA!
THAT'S WHAT I SAID A RAT
HE'S - NOT - A -
WELL, ANYWAY - WHAT D'YOU CALL THE LITTLE FELLA?
JAWS -
YOW!

THIS IS AGENT BEEP CALLING FROM PLANET 53-
KNOWN TO ITS INHABITANTS AS EARTH
NO PROGRESS TO REPORT...
THE NATIVES ARE EXTREMELY SHY-
EEEEK!
THEY RUN AWAY, SCREAMING, AT SIGHT OF ME-
...THEY FEAR ALIENS INORDINATELY....
....AND THEY THINK WE WANT TO CONQUER THEIR PLANET.....
....AND THAT WE'RE A THREAT TO THEIR WAY OF LIFE, THEIR IDEALS, THEIR CUSTOMS....
....AND..... THEY'RE RIGHT.....

IF I SHUT MY EYES VERY TIGHT, THIS HALLUCINATION OF A MARTIAN WILL DISAPPEAR—
NO I WON'T
YES YOU WILL!!
OH ALRIGHT —IF YOU INSIST—
HUH?
LOOK! I'VE DISAPPEARED
AND SO IT HAS—
YUP!
WAITAMINUTE! WHO SAID "YUP"?
I DID
W-WHO ARE YOU??? WH-WHERE ARE YOU?!?
MY NAME IS BEEP—
SHOW YOURSELF AT ONCE, WHOEVER, WHATEVER YOU ARE!
ANYTIME, LADY—
POP
EEEEEEEEK!!
YOU HUMANS ARE IMPOSSIBLE TO PLEASE..
Manjula

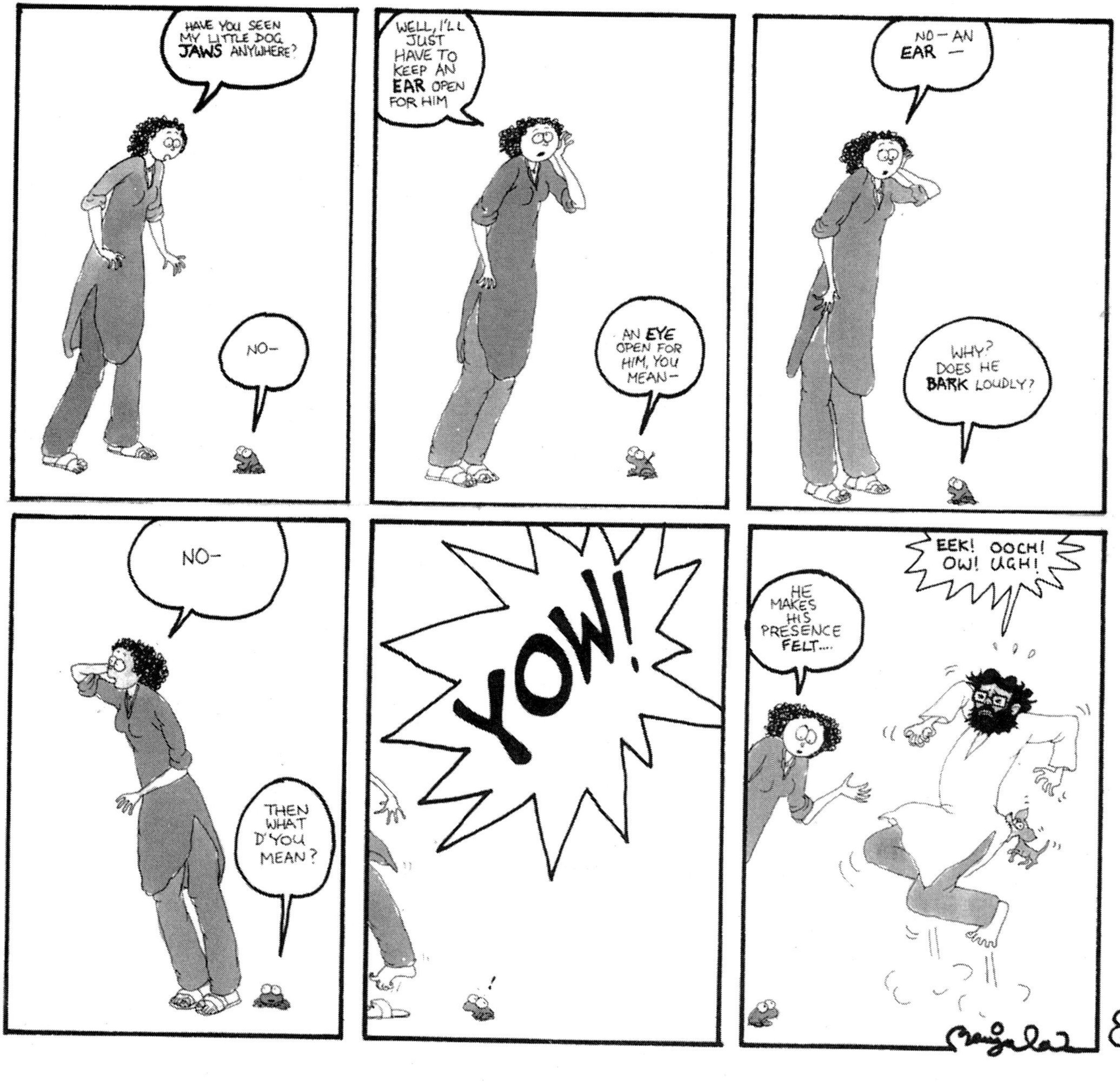
HAVE YOU SEEN MY LITTLE DOG JAWS ANYWHERE?
NO-
WELL, I'LL JUST HAVE TO KEEP AN EAR OPEN FOR HIM
AN EYE OPEN FOR HIM, YOU MEAN-
NO - AN EAR -
WHY? DOES HE BARK LOUDLY?
NO-
THEN WHAT D'YOU MEAN?
YOW!
HE MAKES HIS PRESENCE FELT....
EEK! OOCH! OW! UGH!

OH, GOODY!
IT'S RAINING—
NOW I CAN GROW....
I CAN BECOME A TREE...
I CAN HAVE BRANCHES.... I CAN BEAR FRUIT... I CAN OFFER SHADE...
I CAN SHELTER BIRDS... I CAN HOUSE SQUIRRELS... I CAN...
....UM.....
........BECOME A CORAL REEF?

'SCUSE ME, MS.—
BUT HAVE YOU SEEN SUKI ANYWHERE?
SHE'S RIGHT IN FRONT OF YOU!
SUKI? IS THAT YOU IN THERE?
SHHHH! I'M IN DISGUISE!
DISGUISE?
SHHHHHHHHH! I'M TRYING TO HIDE FROM THE MARTIAN!
IT'S A GOOD DISGUISE!
DON'T TELL THE MARTIAN WHERE I AM!
S'POSE IT'S IN DISGUISE TOO?
NAH! IT'S TOO STUPID!
YOU'RE SURE?
ABSOLUTELY!
UH.....
HULLO, STUPID!

THERE'S NOTHING STANDING ON MY HEAD!
THERE IS!
THERE'S NOTHING STARING ME IN THE FACE...
ACCEPT IT....
MMFFFMM!!
I EXIST!
NOTHING! YEEEEEEESH!
I'M REAL!
NOTHING....
PLEASE NOTICE ME!
NOTHING...
I CAN'T TAKE THIS REJECTION!!
NOTHING...
DON'T DO THIS TO ME!!
...SOMETHING!
SOB!!

SO — YOU'RE SUKI'S PET CHIHUAHUA JAWS—
WELL, LEMME TELL YOU SOMETHING, JAWS—
YOU MAY THINK YOU'RE A DOG, BUT—
— YOU'RE WRONG!!
YOU'RE NOT A DOG, YOU'RE A RAT IN DOG-DISGUISE! YOU'RE A —
ULP!
... UM! .... UH — — THERE'S A NICE DOGGY-WOGGY— 'BYE NOW!
A MOUTHFUL OF TEETH IS WORTH A FISTFUL OF WORDS.....

SUKI?
YES?
WHY ARE YOU STILL WEARING A BURKHA?
I'M ENJOYING IT!
ENJOYING A BURKHA?
WHY NOT?
WHAT'S THERE TO ENJOY?
OH— LOTS OF THINGS
LIKE WHAT F'RINSTANCE?
WELL— IT'S VERY HEALTHY!
HEALTHY?
OH YES—
IN WHAT WAY?
IT GUARDS AGAINST DISEASE...
WHICH DISEASE?
SUN STROKE—

HEY!! WATCH IT!!!
OOPS! SORRY, FROG!!
IT'S OKAY GAUTAM—
IT'S A REALLY DARK NIGHT HUH?
I CAN'T SEE A THING!
WAITAMINUTE! WH-WHAT'S THAT??
WHAT'S WHAT?
TH-THOSE LIGHTS, THERE ...
SIXTEEN LITTLE LIGHTS?
Y-YES!!
OH THAT'S JUST SUKI READING ...
READING?
WITH A TORCH...
UNDER HER BURKHA!
Manjula

HI, SUKI!
HELLO, POET!!
I'VE BEEN TAKING YOUR ADVICE SERIOUSLY...
ADVICE?
ABOUT PLAGIARISM — REMEMBER MY POEM? THE ONE THAT SOUNDS LIKE "DAFFODILS"?
WELL... YES—
REMEMBER YOU TOLD ME TO READ THE ORIGINAL? SO I COULD JUDGE FOR MYSELF?
RIGHT!
AND SO— I DID READ IT—
—AND?
—AND I AGREE, MINE DOES SOUND LIKE "DAFFODILS"!
—AND?
—SO I'VE MADE DRASTIC CHANGES!!
GREAT!! LIKE WHAT?
I'VE CALLED MY POEM "ROSES"!
Manjula

HELLO, FLOWER!
I'M NOT A FLOWER...
NO?
I'M A CORAL REEF
FUNNY- I COULD HAVE SWORN-
APPEARANCES ARE DECEPTIVE
ARE YOU SURE YOU'RE A CORAL REEF?
OH ABSOLUTELY, 100%
WELL! THAT EXPLAINS IT, THEN!!
EXPLAINS WHAT?
IT EXPLAINS WHAT I AM!
AREN'T YOU A BUTTERFLY?
WHY— OF COURSE NOT!!
BUT— WHAT, THEN???
-A SEAGULL
Manjula

SOB!!
!
BAW!!!
WHAT'S THE MATTER, KID?
I'M SO LONELY!!
HUMANS REFUSE TO TALK TO ME!!
THEY ALL RUN AWAY, SCREAMING, AT SIGHT OF ME!
IN FACT, YOU'RE THE FIRST HUMAN TO TALK TO ME DIRECTLY...
YOU MUST BE A VERY SPECIAL BEING!!
W-E-L-L... I DO HAVE ONE GREAT ADVANTAGE
WHAT'S THAT?
I'M NOT HUMAN!!
Mazjula

HOW AMAZING!!
AN EGG
I WONDER WHAT IT'S DOING HERE ALL ALONE
POOR LITTLE EGG!
NO-ONE TO CARE FOR IT! NO-ONE TO HATCH FOR IT! NO-ONE TO LOVE IT! NO-ONE TO....
!
SQUAWK
SNARL!
SNATCH!
....NO-ONE TO EAT IT....
Manjula

GIGGLE GIGGLE GIGGLE!
THESE MATRIMONIAL ADS ARE REALLY HILARIOUS!
HERE'S ONE FROM AN EXTRA-TERRESTRIAL SEEKING HUMAN COMPANIONSHIP—
WHAT A JOKE!
WHO EVER —HEARD— HA HA HA! —OF A—HMMFF! HMMMF! HMMFFF! AN EXTRA-TERRESTRIAL —HEE HEE HEE!— WRITING A —
.....WRITING..... —UHHHHHH— .....WRITING..... ...A ...... A...... M-M-MATRI—
....
EEEEEEEEEEK?

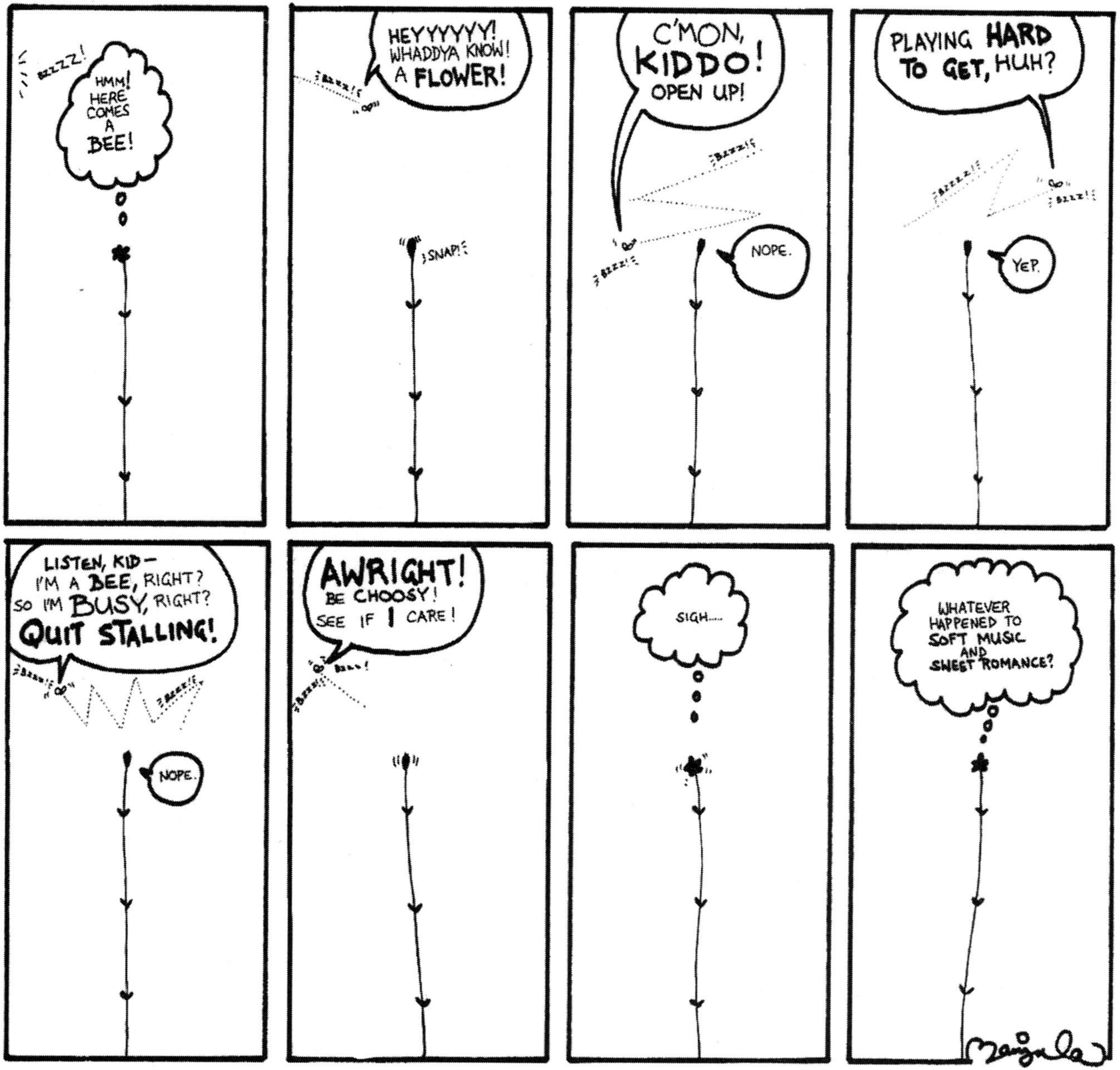
BZZZZ!
HMM! HERE COMES A BEE!
HEYYYYYY! WHADDYA KNOW!! A FLOWER!
SNAP!
C'MON, KIDDO! OPEN UP!
NOPE.
PLAYING HARD TO GET, HUH?
YEP.
LISTEN, KID— I'M A BEE, RIGHT? SO I'M BUSY, RIGHT? QUIT STALLING!
NOPE.
AWRIGHT! BE CHOOSY! SEE IF I CARE!
SIGH....
WHATEVER HAPPENED TO SOFT MUSIC AND SWEET ROMANCE?

I'VE PLACED AN AD IN THE MATRIMONIAL COLUMNS—
"LONELY ALIEN, SHORT (50 cms), BLUE, INTELLECTUAL, WIDELY TRAVELLED, EARNING ASTRONOMICAL SALARY SEEKS COMPANION, PREFERABLY HUMAN, AGE, SEX, NO BAR. MUST BE WARM, LOVING KIND-HEARTED TOWARDS ALIENS. EARLY DECENT FRIENDSHIP. REPLY WITH DETAILS..."
AND??
THE RESPONSE HAS BEEN TREMENDOUS!
REALLY?
I'VE HAD AT LEAST A HUNDRED REPLIES!
AMAZING!
—AND I THOUGHT HUMANS WERE UNFRIENDLY TOWARDS ALIENS!
IT'S QUITE TOUCHING...
THERE'S ONLY ONE THING WHICH PUZZLES ME—
WHAT'S THAT?
THEY ALL INSIST ON ONE MYSTERIOUS QUALIFICATION—
YES?
—WHAT'S A 'GREEN CARD'?
Manjula

THWACK!
THWACK
THWACK
THWACK!
SWISH!
TWACK!
SWISH!
SWISH!
SWISH!
THWACK!
THWACK!
PFFFF!
PANT! PFFFFFF! PANT! PANT!
WATCHA DOING?
BECOMING A JAIN!
Manjula

WHAT'S UP?
I'M MAKING RESOLUTIONS!
RESOLUTIONS?
YOU KNOW - FOR THE NEW YEAR...
A BIT LATE DON'T YOU THINK?
LATE? NO - WHY?
1986 IS ALREADY TWO SUNDAYS OLD!!
OH SURE -
- BUT THIS IS NEXT YEAR'S LIST!
Manjula

HI SUKI!
HELLO, POET!
GUESS WHAT!
WHAT?
I'VE WRITTEN A GREAT POEM!!
REALLY?
SHALL I READ IT TO YOU?
SURE
AHEM!
"IN XANADU DID KUBLA KHAN A STATELY PLEASURE DOME DECREE ...."
STOP!!
WHY?
THAT'S A VERY WELL-KNOWN POEM CALLED-
-YOU SEE?!!
HUH?
- FAMOUS EVEN BEFORE I WROTE IT!!
Manjula

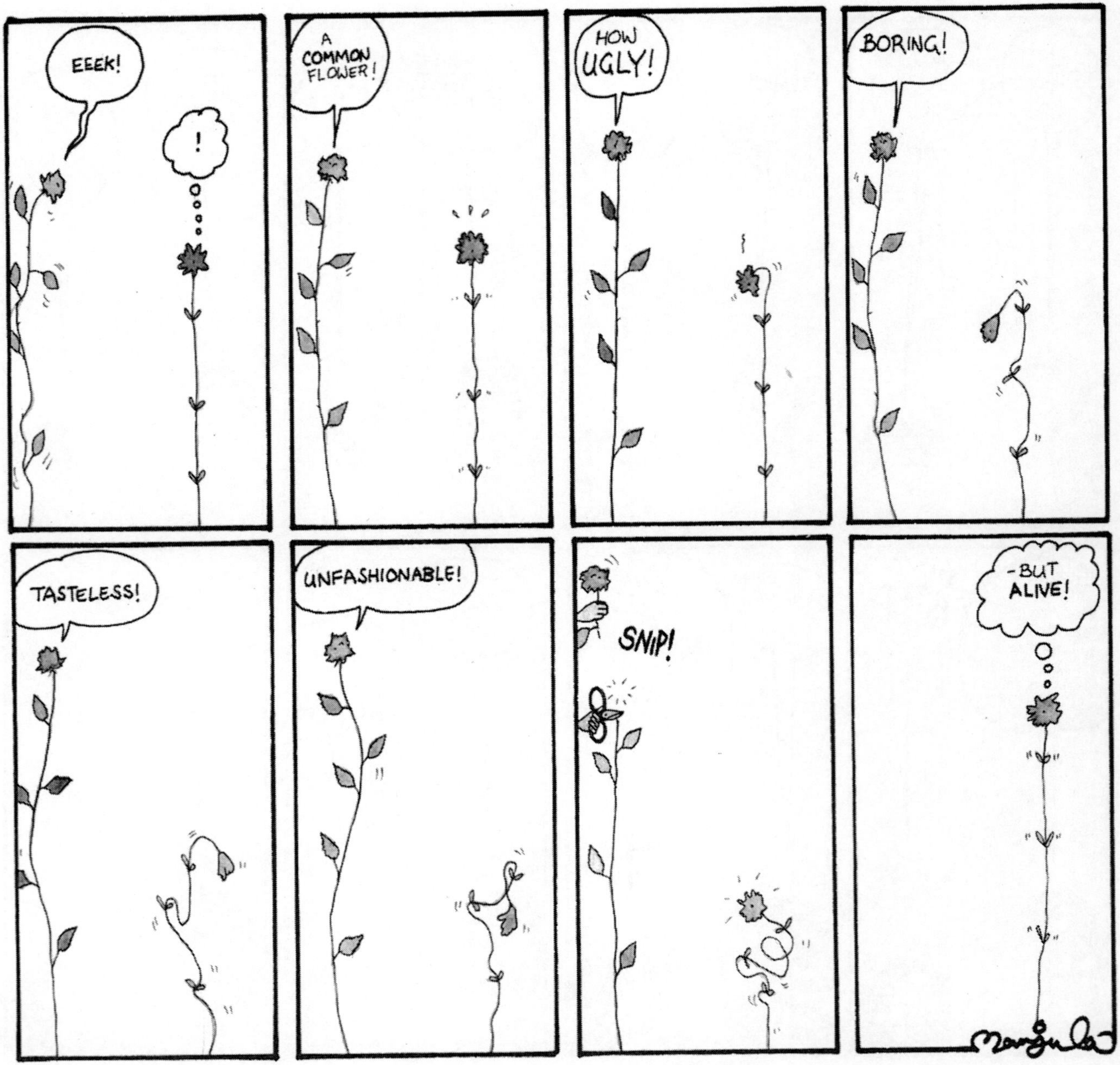
EEEK!
!
A COMMON FLOWER!
HOW UGLY!
BORING!
TASTELESS!
UNFASHIONABLE!
SNIP!
-BUT ALIVE!

NOW THAT YOU'VE ACKNOWLEDGED MY PRESENCE...
WE CAN ENGAGE IN CULTURAL EXCHANGES!!
OUR PLANETS HAVE MUCH TO LEARN FROM ONE ANOTHER...
... AS WE EMBARK ON THIS UNIQUE ADVENTURE....
WE MUST CHOOSE OUR WORDS CAREFULLY...
THE FATE OF THE UNIVERSE ITSELF COULD DEPEND ON OUR DISCUSSIONS!!
SO— WHAT DO YOU SAY, EARTHLING SUKI!?
JUST TO BE ON THE SAFE SIDE, HOW ABOUT...
GOOD BYE ?

Manjula

OUCH!
JAWS! IT'S YOU AGAIN, HUH?
WELL LET ME TELL YOU SOMETHING, JAWS....
WHISPER WHISPER WHISPER
HA! HA HA! HA HA HA!
HEE HEE
HO HO
HO HO
HA! HA
?
WHAT'S SO FUNNY?
WOW! I REALLY FIXED YOUR STUPID LITTLE DOG!!
HOW?
I SCARED THE DAYLIGHTS OUT OF HIM!!
WHAT'D YOU DO?!?
I TOLD HIM I HAD RABIES!

SUKI!!
HOW ARE YOU, DARLING?
SMACK!
I-
I'M FINE!!
UH-
DON'T I LOOK WONDERFUL?
...UM...
ALL THE LATEST FASHIONS, ALL THE.... OOOH!!
WASSAMATTER?
SOB!! MY NAILPOLISH HAS CHIPPED!!!
......
SEE YOU LATER DARLING...
-WOMEN!
manjula

HI SUKI- HAVE YOU SEEN THE NEWS-?
NAH! IT'S TOO DEPRESSING!
BUT- AREN'T YOU INTERESTED IN THE FATE OF THE WORLD?
OH POOH! IT CAN TAKE CARE OF ITSELF!
REALLY? HOW ABOUT-
DON'T TELL ME! I DON'T WANT TO BE DEPRESSED!
HMMMM! INTERESTING!
WHAT IS?
YOUR VIEWPOINT...
A BIT SELF-CENTRED BUT- HEY!!! WHAT'S THE MATTER?
OH- NOTHING!
WHY ARE YOU DUCKING?
NO REASON!
THERE MUST BE SOME REASON-
YES- BUT IT'S A LITTLE DEPRESSING...
Manjula